Rug Weaving

Plate 1 *Part-tufted Rug* (*p.* 107)
Designed and woven by Helen Hutton

Rug
Weaving

Klares Lewes
& Helen Hutton

CHARLES T. BRANFORD COMPANY
NEWTON CENTRE 59, MASSACHUSETTS

First published in the United States of America 1962

Printed and bound in Great Britain by Jarrold and Sons Ltd, London and Norwich

CONTENTS

		Page
INTRODUCTION		9
ACKNOWLEDGMENT		11
LIST OF PLATES		13

Chapter

1   **The Loom and its Accessories**   15

    The Horizontal Loom   19
    The Upright Loom   21
    The Rug Frame Loom   21
    Accessories   29

2   **Materials and Calculations of Quantities**   37

    The Warp   37
    Weft Materials   38
    Calculation of Quantities   43

3   **Preparing the Loom**   45

    Laying the Warp   45
    Multi-coloured Warp   47
    Chaining the Warp   48
    'Beaming On'   49
    Raddling   49
    Rolling On   50
    Threading Up   54
    Reeding   55
    The Tie-up   55
    Points to Remember   58

4   **Basic Principles of Weaving. Draft Reading**   60

    Draft Reading   63
    Twill   66
    Rosepath   67
    Honeycomb   69
    Double-woven Rugs   76
    Spot Pattern   79
    Points to Remember   80

Chapter		Page
5	Rag Rugs	82
6	Tufted Rugs	87
	Cut Length Method	88
	Short Pile Method	91
	Rya *and* Flossa *Rugs*	93
	Imitation Flossa *or Overshot Pattern*	93
7	Finishing Off	95
	Points to Remember	98
8	Design	101
9	Notes on the Plates	107
	Appendix: A Home-made Loom	143
	BIBLIOGRAPHY	151
	LIST OF SUPPLIERS	152
	GLOSSARY	153
	INDEX	156

List of Some Suppliers in the United States and Canada

BARTLETT MILLS, INC., Harmony, Maine.

2-ply Harmony Grade 100% wool, substitute for 2-ply carpet wool.

All wool rug yarn, substitute for 6-ply rug wool.

BRIGGS & LITTLE

York Mills, Harvey Station P. O., York Co., N. B., Canada.
2/6 wool, substitute for 2-ply carpet wool.

6-ply rug wool, substitute for 6-ply rug wool.

WM. CONDON & SONS

65 Queen St., Charlottetown, P.E.I., Canada.

3-ply coarse, substitute for 2-ply carpet wool.

5-ply wool, substitute for 6-ply rug wool.

COUNTRYSIDE HANDWEAVERS, Mission, Kansas.

8/4 linen warp, substitute for linen rug warp.

2-ply Flossa, substitute for 2-ply carpet wool.

2-ply Flossa (use double), substitute for 6-ply rug wool.

HOUSE OF KLEEN, Essex, Conn.

Afgahn-Garn (use double), substitute for 2-ply carpet wool.

Frosta-Garn (use double), substitute for 6-ply rug wool.

8/4 linen warp, substitute for linen rug warp.

LILY MILLS, Shelby, N. C.

8/5 linen warp, substitute for linen rug warp.

8-cord cable twist or 4/4 heavy carpet warp, substitutes for 10/6 cotton twine.

PATERNAYAN BROS., INC.,

312 E. 95th St., New York 28, N. Y.

Paterna Persian (use double), substitute for 2-ply carpet wool.

Pat rug yarn, substitute for 6-ply rug wool.

GEORGE WELLS, The Ruggery, Glen Head, Long Island, N. Y.

3-ply fine (oyster, natural cream, white), substitute for 2-ply carpet wool.

3-ply heavy rug yarn (above colors, plus antique black) or 4-ply medium (use double) oyster only, substitutes for 6-ply rug wool.

Yarns called for in this book are available from English firms. Substitutes suggested are approximate in size, in some instances texture and quality may not be similar.

The writer does not know of suitable substitutes for English wool warp yarns: 4/5½s camel hair, 4/6s white wool warp, and 4/5½s grey wool.

ERRATA

Page 55. A reference under "The Tie-Up" *should be* "warp tie-up (Fig. 17c)," not "simple reef-knot (Fig. 17a)."

Page 97, paragraph beginning "To finish off the fringe." Both instructions and illustration are in error. For yarns with an S-twist the initial twist should be to the right, and the second to the left.

SUGGESTIONS

The treadle tie-ups are for looms with sinking sheds. For rising shed looms tie up opposite harnesses from those indicated herein.

Referring to the top of page 97, the final last three pairs of warp ends could be plaited into a short braid, knotted at the end for security.

INTRODUCTION

THIS BOOK ATTEMPTS to teach a craft. In stating its purpose, we indicate our approach. Rug-weaving is a craft, and crafts are a strictly practical form of human activity. First comes the desire to make something, that is, to be creative, and the idea what that something is to be. Thereafter everything is practical, concrete, the problem of translating the idea into solid form, which is a matter of materials and how to handle them—in short, technique.

In this book we have sought to be strictly practical, avoiding history, sentimental disquisitions on the craftsmen of old, abstract theorising on aesthetics.

Though in fact not so divided, the book falls into two parts, the first part —Chapters 1 to 7—concerned with the techniques of rug-weaving, the second with 'worked examples'.

Throughout we rely upon drawings and photographs, for the subject is one which is easy to demonstrate, not so easy to explain in words that will leave no loophole for error and misunderstanding. Throughout, too, we have done our best to anticipate the practical difficulties that will inevitably arise from time to time when things do not go exactly 'according to the book'.

The worked examples consist of photographs of a number of rugs by various designers, and represent both simple and advanced work. Most of them can be copied by following the weaving instructions which accompany them. They can be given a wholly different character by being woven in different colour schemes, or by varying the arrangement of the weave pattern in ways which, with a little experience, will readily suggest themselves to the reader. They can be used to produce original designs by combining elements of one with elements of another in the same or in alternative colours.

The question of originality brings us back to our starting-point, which is the idea. This, when given solid form, becomes the design. But no idea, and no design, just happens. Always there is something else which suggests it, consciously or subconsciously. To illustrate this we have included some photographs of natural objects together with the rugs whose design they have inspired. It is by learning to look for and convert to his own use the possibilities which even quite commonplace objects may contain, that the merely competent worker develops into the creative craftsman.

For those who wish to construct their own loom and thereby effect a quite considerable saving on the cost of their equipment, we have added an Appendix of necessary drawings and instructions based on two of our looms which are home-built. The skill required is that of the ordinary amateur wood-worker. The loom chosen is a 4-shaft 6-pedal loom, on which any kind of rug-weaving can be carried out. The size is 4 feet, satisfactory for most purposes, but this can easily be modified to produce a larger or smaller loom to suit individual requirements.

ACKNOWLEDGMENT

WE OWE THANKS for assistance received in generous measure, in particular from those rug designers, many of them complete strangers to us though their names of course are well known, who readily gave permission to reproduce examples of their work, and added to their kindness by supplying where possible—that is to say, where memory served or notes had been kept—the necessary weaving instructions: Tadek Beutlich, Peter Collingwood, Marlene Frühoff, Ronald Grierson, F.S.I.A., Brian Knight, DES. R.C.A., F.R.S.A., Anne Meurling, Rodney Moorhouse, DES. R.C.A., F.R.S.A., Mrs. E. G. Mullins, Barbara Mullins, Mary Patten, CERT. DES. R.C.A., Marianne Straub, F.S.I.A.

We wish to express our gratitude to the following for permission to reproduce certain illustrations:

Robin Day, R.D.I., A.R.C.S., F.S.I.A., for plate 30.

Liberty & Co., for plates 11 and 41.

John Maxwell, for plates 2 and 3.

Pamela Pearce, for the photograph of plate 45.

THE PLATES

Plate		Page
1	*Part–tufted rug*	*Frontispiece*
2	*Horizontal overslung loom*	17
3	*Upright rug loom*	17
4	*Section of loom showing shafts and heddles supported by castle*	18
5	*Threading the heddles*	18
6	*The warp reeded and partly attached to the cloth roller*	18
7	*Skein winder*	25
8	*Spool holder*	25
9	*Warping mill and spool holder*	26
10	*Sample warp–faced weave*	35
11	*Tufted hemp rug*	35
12	*Rya rug, 'Stained Window'*	36
13	*Wool rug showing Oriental fringe completed at one end*	41
14	*Rush mat*	41
15	*Sample wool rug weave*	41
16	*Making the Parrey Cross*	42
17	*Securing the cross*	42
18	*Chaining the warp*	51
19	*Warp secured by cloth stick*	51
20	*The warp raddled*	52
21	*Reeding*	52
22	*Sample rag rug weave in twill*	61
23	*Sample rug in Goose–eye*	61

Plate		Page
24	Sample rug in Rosepath and Tabby	62
25	Sample rag rug weave with spot pattern	62
26, 27, 28	Wool rug in Honeycomb weave, inspired by a dry stone wall in Cornwall	71
29	Wool rug in Rosepath and Tabby	72
30, 31	Khelim type rug, the design based on a dining-room furniture set	77
32	Rag rug in Tabby and Rosepath	78
33	Experimental rug using three twist methods	78
34	Rag rug with inlay pattern	83
35, 36	Rag rugs with inlay pattern	84
37, 38	Tapestry and tufted rugs	89
39	Rya rug	90
40, 41	Tufted rugs	99
42	Sample weave in imitation Flossa	100
43	Rya rug	100
44, 45	A tufted rug, inspired by a volcanic pool	105
46	Rug in double weave	106
47	Rug in double weave	115
48, 49	Chequered rug in Rosepath and Tabby, based on a pebble and brick pavement	116
50	Tapestry rug	129
51	Rya rug	130
52, 53	Khelim rugs	139
54	Warp and weft rug, 'Black and White'	140

CHAPTER ONE

The Loom and its Accessories

IF YOU LOOK closely at a section of woven material, you will see that it consists of two sets of threads interlaced crosswise at right angles (Fig. 1). The threads running lengthways along the weave are known collectively as the 'warp'; those running across from selvedge to selvedge are called the 'weft'.

It is the interlacing of these threads which constitutes the process of weaving, a process used not only for producing cloth, but also all kinds of rugs other than the knotted and the hooked rug; and even in these there is an element of weaving.

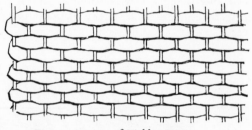

Fig. 1. Section of Tabby Weave

The main equipment needed for it is a loom which basically is no more than a rigid rectangular frame. The warp threads, evenly spaced, are stretched from one side to the opposite side, and the weft threads can then be woven in by interlacing them one at a time with the warp threads. This is weaving at its most primitive and as a method it suffers from several drawbacks which will be overcome in a more advanced loom. How, then, is this done?

In the first place, it is obvious that with a simple frame one cannot produce a weave larger than the frame itself. This difficulty is met by equipping two opposite sides of the frame with a long roller each, fitted with a ratchet wheel to enable its turning to be controlled. The warp is wound on to one of the rollers, and its free end taken across the frame and attached to the other roller. Then as the work proceeds the warp can gradually be unwound from the first roller and the finished weave wound on to the second roller; in this way it becomes possible to produce pieces of any length within reason.

The second problem is the interlacing of the weft threads. This would be a slow and tiresome task if one had to work the weft through the warp thread by thread, over or under, one at a time (though as a matter of fact this primitive process is one still used with beautiful results, amongst for example the Navajo Indians in North America). Moreover, working in this way one could only produce the simplest weave pattern, the so-called 'tabby'; anything more complicated, such as 'twill' or a 'herringbone' weave, would be impractical.

The solution is to pass each warp thread through a short length of looped string called a 'heddle'. The loops are suspended in sets from sticks, known as heddle-holders or shafts, so that if one stick is raised it will lift with it a whole series of warp threads, separating them from the remainder. This separation is termed a 'shed' (Fig. 2) and it obviously makes it easy to pass a shuttle carrying the weft yarn from one side of the warp straight through to the other in such a way that some of the warp threads will be over, and the rest under the weft. All that it is necessary to do is to pass the shuttle through the shed. Interlacing is now automatic. And if the heddles have been arranged correctly on their holders, then there can be no possibility of a mistake in the weave.

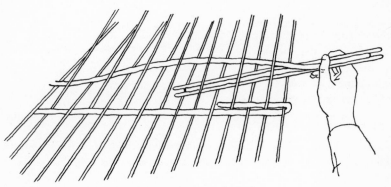

Fig. 2. Section of Shed

The lifting of the heddles can be done either by a simple hand control or by a foot pedal arrangement. The sets of heddles and shafts can be two in number—all that is required for a plain tabby weave—or three, four, six or even eight or twelve for the more elaborate weave patterns. In rug-making four shafts is the most common number, but six or eight are occasionally used to produce an even greater variety of patterns.

Lastly come the 'batten' or beater and the 'reed'. It will be appreciated that in order to be serviceable a rug must be as closely woven as possible, which means that the weft threads must be pressed together as closely as possible: in many cases indeed they will actually be pressed together so closely as to cover

Plate 2 Horizontal Overslung Loom

Plate 3 Upright Rug Loom

Plate 4 Section of Loom showing Shafts and Heddles supported by Castle

Plate 5 Threading the Heddles

Plate 6 The Warp reeded and partly attached to the Cloth Roller

the warp threads completely on back and front and will thus protect them from wear. All this is achieved by means of a reed, a metal construction looking rather like a large comb with covered points, attached to a heavy wooden beam which is the batten. The warp is threaded through the reed, which thus serves the additional purpose of spacing the threads evenly. The batten is pivoted somewhere on the frame in such a way that it can be brought forward with considerable force (but little expenditure of energy) against the weft threads, thus compressing them together.

Looms are made both as table and as floor models. The table model, however, is hardly suitable for rug-making since its batten is not heavy enough to deal with the thick materials used in rugs, nor would its light framework stand the strain.

The floor models include two main types, the horizontal and the upright. Both are made in different sizes, the reference here being to the width of the frame. This is the key dimension, for on it depends the maximum width of weave which can be produced. From this point of view it would seem that the larger the frame, the better, but then considerations of available space come into the picture. Looms can take up a great deal of room, which has to be found somewhere. Moreover it is not every day that one will wish to produce a 6 ft. carpet: the normal requirement is much more likely to be a 3 ft. rug. One adequate for the latter will therefore normally be a more reasonable proposition, and here it should be borne in mind that it is perfectly feasible to weave two or more narrow widths and join them together in exactly the same way as a 'made-up' carpet is built up.

One thing to bear in mind when choosing a loom is that the frame width may be deceptive. If the roller ratchet wheels are on the inside of the frame instead of on the outside, they will detract from the width available for weaving so that due allowance for this must be made.

THE HORIZONTAL LOOM

This is made in two main patterns, the 'overslung' (Plate 2) and the 'under-slung' (Fig. 3). The reference here is to the batten which in the former is suspended from the top of the frame, in the latter pivoted from the base. Choice as between them is probably a matter of individual taste. Adherents of the overslung will claim that it enables one to develop a more rhythmic 'swing', and has the added advantage that extra weights are easily attached to it if it is not heavy enough. Those who favour the other type will point out that the overslung beam merely rests in a groove, from which it can jump out with over-enthusiastic beating and fall on to the weaver's head; they will also claim that the underslung batten is as easily weighted as the overslung. The truth is that there is no real difference between the two and it is all a matter of 'what you're used to'.

The loom chosen should be substantially made and heavy, for the strain on it will be considerable. The warp threads must be very taut, which means

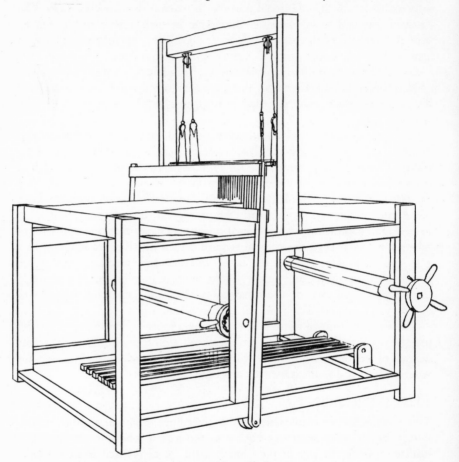

Fig. 3. Horizontal Underslung Loom

a strain of several pounds per thread: multiply this by the number of threads, say 288 for a 3 ft. rug woven at 8 threads to the inch, and the result will be a pull amounting to the best part of a ton. Add the shock forces of the beating, which must be heavy and vigorous, and it will be seen why only very solid timber will stand up to the work.

20

Naturally such looms are fairly expensive to buy, though it is often possible to find a second-hand one advertised at a modest price, in a crafts magazine or even—for country-dwellers—in the local paper. However, if there is a handyman about the house then it will be infinitely better to have a loom built to one's own requirements. The standard of carpentry needed is not very high and the cost of materials only about a quarter of the price of a shop-bought loom. To assist we have included an appendix with simplified plans and all necessary instructions.

THE UPRIGHT LOOM

This, the second main type of loom, is altogether simpler in construction than the horizontal type (Plate 3). Seen from the side it looks rather like ordinary household steps, the front portion in this case being the weaving frame and the rear the support. The frame is fitted with rollers at top and bottom, the continuous warp being secured to the top roller and the finished weave wound on to the bottom roller. Heddles, with or without foot pedal operation, are provided, as is a batten and reed.

It has the limitation that it cannot be equipped with more than two shafts so that the only weave possible is the tabby. Thus the only purpose of pedal control is to speed the shed change. However, because it stands upright this loom does offer what some people consider a more convenient working position, and it is extremely suitable for making hand-tufted rugs and woven rugs (such as Khelims), which depend for their effect upon colour design alone and not upon weave pattern.

A further advantage is that the upright loom takes up much less space than the horizontal loom, an important consideration when space is a factor, as it often is.

THE RUG FRAME LOOM

This is the simplest kind of loom in use today, and one that is hardly distinguishable from the loom in its most primitive form (Fig. 4). It consists merely of a solid wooden frame having two heavy lengths of wood fastened by thumbscrews to the top and bottom sides. These form clamps to grip the warp at the top and the finished weave at the bottom. Instead of heddles one uses 'leashes', which are really the same thing with the same function. They are operated by hand to form the shed, and this is maintained by inserting a 'shed stick' and turning it on edge so as to keep the shed open. In Khelim pattern weaving these leashes are lifted in groups by hand enabling small areas of pattern to be worked at a time.

The illustrations of these various looms show clearly their general differences. For a detailed description we will take the horizontal loom (Fig. 3), which is the most useful type for rug-making.

As already mentioned, a loom is basically a heavy wooden framework of solid construction. It is made in sections which can easily be taken apart for moving and storing. To prevent movement in use, some weavers will fasten

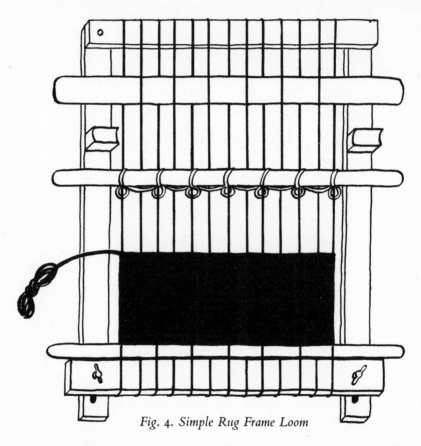

Fig. 4. Simple Rug Frame Loom

it permanently to the floor or screw a block of wood in front of each foot. A simpler solution is to place a piece of 2 in. or thicker sponge rubber under each foot; this is sufficient to prevent forward jumps as one beats the weave and will also deaden noise.

The frame carries two rollers 4 inches in diameter or more running parallel at front and back, each fitted with a toothed wheel and ratchet so that the

22

rollers can be turned in either direction for winding or unwinding but locked in position when the correct warp tension has been found.

As there is considerable strain on the rollers, it is most important that the ratchets should be kept in good condition and replaced when the teeth become worn.

Attached to each roller is a strip of stout linen canvas or calico known as the 'roller cloth'. The free end of the cloth has a wide hem open either side into which is inserted a wooden rod or lath. To this another rod or lath known as the 'roller stick' is tied at intervals, and serves to hold the warp in the case of the back roller and the finished weave in the case of the front roller. The purpose of this arrangement is to make the attachment of the warp easy and to ensure an even distribution of the strain over the whole width of the warp.

The warp threads on their journey from back roller to front pass first through the heddles and then through the reed.

The heddles are merely short lengths of cotton twine knotted so as to form three loops. Heddles can also be obtained which are made of thin wire, and these presumably will last indefinitely. The top and bottom loops are slipped over the heddle holders or shafts and the warp thread is passed through the centre loop.

Cotton heddles can easily be made at home on a simple jig consisting of four nails in line driven into a piece of scrap wood (Fig. 5). Use of such a jig ensures that all the heddles will be of exactly the same overall length and size of loop. The actual dimensions used are not critical: a suitable length would be 12 inches, the centre loop being, say, 2 inches long and the outer loop 5 inches each.

The total number required will depend upon the width of the rug and the density of the warp used. Thus a rug 36 inches wide with a warp at 8 threads to the inch would have $8 \times 36 = 288$ warp threads (without allowance for selvedge) and would thus require 288 heddles.

As mentioned, the heddles are threaded on to heddle shafts which are simply wooden laths, one passing through the upper loop of the heddle, and the other through the bottom, the whole arrangement constituting a 'heddle shaft'.

The number of heddle shafts used is never less than two and may be as many as eight for rug-weaving, depending upon the complexity of the weave patterns one wishes to produce. (For cloth-weaving the number may even far exceed this.) With two, the weaver is limited to the simplest weave, the tabby. Four shafts (Plate 4) will extend the range considerably and are probably all that is required.

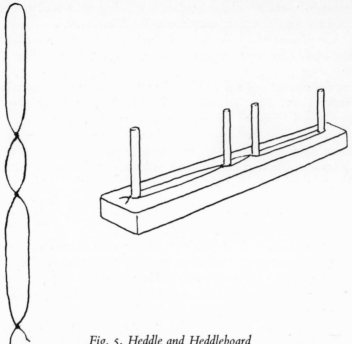

Fig. 5. Heddle and Heddleboard

The heddles are distributed among the shafts according to a definite scheme depending on the weave pattern. The frames themselves are suspended from the upper cross-bar of the loom by a connected pulley system so arranged that when certain frames are raised, others will be lowered. By the same token certain groups of warp threads will be raised and others lowered, this producing the separation between them referred to as the 'shed', through which the weft thread is passed.

The raising and lowering is effected by means of pedals to which the lower bars of the heddle shafts are connected, usually by being tied to an intermediate bar called a lam which is in turn tied to the appropriate pedal. The lams are of course pivoted at one end so that the free end can move up and down (Fig. 6).

The lams are at first sight an unnecessary elaboration. With a simple two-shaft system they are in fact not needed. With a four or more shaft system however they make it possible to connect different combinations of shafts to the various pedals, for although there must be one lam to each shaft, each

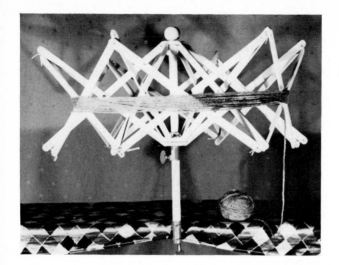

Plate 7 Skein Winder

Plate 8 Spool Holder

Plate 9 *Warping Mill and Spool Holder*

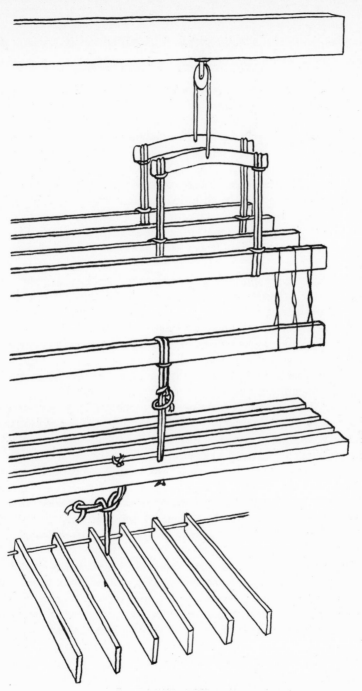

Fig. 6. Arrangement of Shafts, Lams and Pedals in a Four-Shaft Six-Pedal Loom

lam can be tied to two or more pedals. It is a simple device, but it is the one which makes possible the innumerable draft patterns that a weaver can produce.

The arrangement of the warp threads on the various heddle shafts is known as the 'thread-up'; the combination of shafts, lams and pedals as the 'pedal tie-up'. These two things, plus the order of operating the pedals, will always be given in weave designs: they are the vital instructions, for only by knowing the thread-up, the tie-up and the pedalling order is it possible to reproduce a weave pattern.

To return to the warp threads. Having been threaded through the heddles (Plate 5), they must next be threaded through the reed (Plate 6) which we have already described as a kind of steel comb with the teeth covered. The reed rests in a groove on the batten and is retained in position by means of a moveable grooved bar. It can thus be taken off and changed quite easily.

The reed can be bought in lengths to suit the length of the batten. When ordering one it is necessary also to specify the spacing between the teeth, which is known as the 'dentage', on the basis of 'dents' to the inch. The choice (within very broad limits) depends on the fineness or coarseness of the warp thread and the type of weave. An average dentage for rugs is four to the inch, though for something really heavy three, or even two, might be used. With a lighter warp and weft, and perhaps a more complex design and weave pattern, six or eight dents to the inch might be more suitable.

Although different dentages are used for different warps and weaves, this does not mean that one must buy a whole set of reeds. An eight-dent reed, for instance, will serve perfectly well as a four-dent reed if only alternate dents are threaded (provided of course that the warp is not so thick that it does not run freely through the dents). Similarly, a six-dent reed can be used as a three-dent or a two-dent reed.

The last stage is the attachment of the warp to the front roller. As with the attachment to the back roller, this is done by tying the warp threads in small groups to a rod or lath which is itself tied to a roller cloth fastened to the roller (Plate 6).

In its passage from reed to front roller the warp, which in due course becomes the weave, passes over the front beam of the loom, usually known as the breast beam. Since weavers tend to lean forward against this, and so may rub against and mark the finished weave as it passes over the breast beam, a protection is often provided in the shape of a wooden slat known as the breast batten in front of the breast beam. This slat is simply slotted into grooves to allow of easy fixing and removal.

ACCESSORIES

Most of the accessory equipment needed is simple and inexpensive, and can be improvised if desired.

When preparing a warp—which may be 10 or 20 yards long and consist of two or three hundred threads—entanglement is an obvious risk, especially since it is usual, in order to speed the work, to take the thread from as many as half-a-dozen or more balls (or cops) simultaneously.

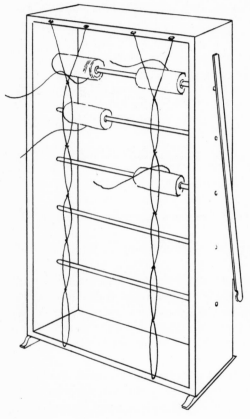

Fig. 7. Spool Holder

A *spool holder* ensures tidiness at this stage (Fig. 7, Plate 8). This is a simple wooden frame with the uprights bored at suitable spacing to receive a number of $\frac{1}{4}$-in. iron rods upon which the cops can be held. The dimensions of the frame do not matter so long as there is room on the bars for a convenient number of cops.

The threads are led from the spool holder to a *warping board* or *warping mill*. The former (Fig. 7) is the simpler and takes up less space since it can be used on a table or hung from a wall; but it is not suitable for warps more than about 10 yards in length. It consists of a wooden board an inch thick and measuring about 36 in. × 24 in., into which lengths of $\frac{1}{2}$ inch dowelling are pegged. The pegs hold the warp which is wound back and forth between them (Fig. 8a and b).

The *warping mill* (Plate 9) is a more elaborate affair which can take any size of warp and is very convenient in use. It occupies a good deal of space, but is made to be taken apart for stowing away. It consists of a skeleton box frame mounted vertically by means of diagonal cross-bars on to a standing

29

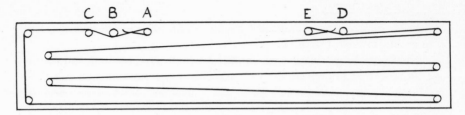

Fig. 8a. Warping Board: First Thread Laid

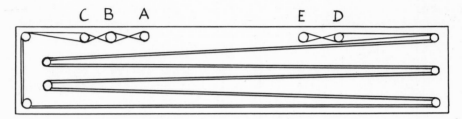

Fig. 8b. Warping Board: Second Thread Laid

axle on which it can turn quite freely. The usual size is about 6 ft. high with 3 ft. sides. Like the warping board it has a number of pegs between which the warp is wound, in this case however simply by spinning the mill round with one hand while guiding the threads with the other. It is very quick in use, since one turn of the mill can put on as much as six yards of thread.

When the warp has been prepared it is wound on to the back roller of the loom. The winding must be as tight as possible, and in order to ensure that individual threads in upper layers should not cut into lower layers, which would produce an uneven warp tension, it is necessary to keep the layers separate by inserting wooden laths between them. Two dozen or so of *rolling-on sticks* should therefore be obtained, of a length almost equal to that of the roller, and measuring about $1\frac{1}{4}$ inch in width by $\frac{1}{4}$ inch thickness.

In addition two *shed sticks* will be needed. The warp is split into two groups of threads and the purpose of the shed sticks, which are inserted in the warp as it comes off the back roller, is to maintain this split. The shed sticks are exactly the same as the rolling-on sticks, save that a hole is drilled at each end to enable a piece of string to be stretched along the length and tied. This serves to prevent the shed stick from slipping out of place.

As a help in drawing the warp threads through the reed, one uses a *reed hook* (Fig. 9), which is a brass or aluminium strip some 5–6 inches long with a hook shaped in each end.

To ensure that the warp is spread evenly across the back roller, it must be passed through a raddle (Plate 19). This is in effect a wooden comb dented 2 to the inch, which is tied in place of the reed during the rolling-on process. A satisfactory raddle can be made by hammering 3 inch nails into a $1\frac{1}{2} \times 1\frac{1}{2}$ inch batten so as to leave about 2 inches of the nails projecting.

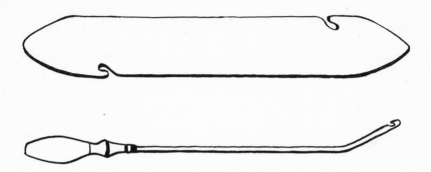

Fig. 9. Two Types of Reed Hook

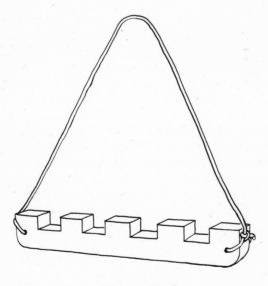

Fig. 10. Castle

The *castles* (Fig. 10) are two short wooden holders which serve to support the heddle shafts during the threading-up process. The name comes from the appearance, square notches in which the shafts rest being cut in one edge of each holder.

The equipment discussed so far relates entirely to the handling of the warp. The weft makes fewer demands. The only essential equipment, in fact, is a

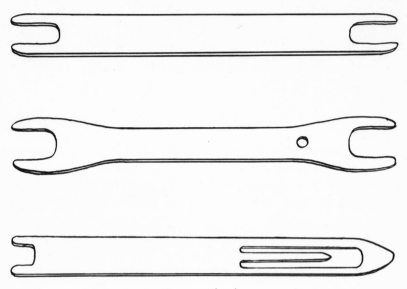

Fig. 11. *Shuttles*

few shuttles (Fig. 11). For most kinds of rugs the rather primitive type shown at the top is suitable. This consists of a flat wooden stick notched at each end to retain the yarn which is wound on to the shuttle. A two-foot shuttle is a good average length for throwing across a 30 or 36 inch warp, and can indeed be used for narrower warps, though a shorter shuttle would probably be more convenient.

For Khelim and interlock types of rugs, the shuttle shown at the bottom is perhaps the best, and it will save time if as many shuttles are available as the colours employed. However, if one has a spool winder one can dispense with shuttles and make do with small spools of thread wound on paper cores or bobbins. These will be found perfectly adequate. Simpler still, though not quite so convenient is to make up 'dollies' by winding the threads into small balls.

32

Spool winders can be obtained in various designs, a good one being illustrated in Fig. 12. A short length of paper is wound on to the spindle, the end of the weft caught in a fold, and the thread guided on to the paper as the handle is turned. When sufficient thread has been wound, the finished bobbin can be slipped off the spindle.

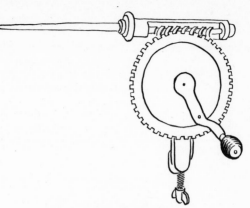

Fig. 12. Spool Winder

For converting skeins of wool into balls, a skein winder saves time. Any pattern will do, but a handy table model is illustrated on Plate 7.

For tufting rugs a tufting gauge is indispensable. This is merely a short length of wood or metal of a width equal to the length of tuft required. The wool is wound on to this closely and then cut into the correct lengths by

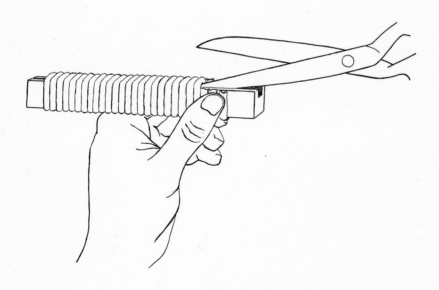

Fig. 13. Tufting Gauge

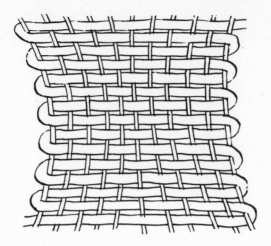

Fig. 14. Waisted Weave

running a razor-blade or a pair of scissors down one edge (Fig. 13). Tufting gauges can be bought in various widths, and will probably have a groove down one edge to facilitate cutting with scissors. They can also be made up at home as required, using smooth scrap wood.

Whether for tufting or weaving rugs, a *template* will be found invaluable. Its purpose is to maintain a constant width in the weave, so counteracting a natural tendency to tighten which, if unchecked, will produce a 'waisted' weave (Fig. 14). The template (Fig. 15) consists of two wood or metal bars

Fig. 15. Template

locked together in such a way that the overall length can be adjusted to the width of the weave. Its two ends are equipped with stout steel teeth like old-fashioned gramophone needles which are pressed into the edges of the weave. The template must of course be moved up as the work proceeds, say every 5–6 inches, since only if it is kept fairly close to the working edge of the rug will it perform its function.

We have not mentioned scissors or tape-measure. They are as vital as the loom itself.

34

Plate 10 *Sample Warp-faced Weave* (p. 107)

Plate 11 *Tufted Hemp Rug* (p. 107)
Designed and woven by Rodney Moorhouse

Plate 12 Rya *Rug*, 'Stained *Window*' (*p.* 93)
Designed and woven by Tadek Beutlich

CHAPTER TWO

Materials and Calculations of Quantities

THE RANGE OF materials that can be turned to successful use in a weave of one kind or another is enormous. Thus, we once returned from a seaside trip with a load of flotsam found on the beach, rushes and long, narrow, very thin and flexible strips of some unknown wood. With the addition of some bamboo sticks taken from the garden and some strips of cotton material torn from an old dress, they were woven into some very effective wall hangings and window blinds. One should have a bit of fun with one's weaving. Besides, one should always be ready to experiment in order to discover new effects and avoid stagnation. An adventuresome example of this is the plumber's hemp normally used to help seal water-pipe joints, but here to make the rug shown on Plate 11.

Before experiment can start, however, one must be thoroughly familiar with the basic materials and it is these that we propose to discuss here. One general point however, both obvious and often overlooked, should be made by way of introduction. A good rug is not merely one that looks attractive by reason of its colour and design, but one that will wear well, and wear well in its particular circumstances. Consequently to produce a good rug one must use materials suitable for the job. What is highly necessary in a hall rug will not be needed in a bedroom or a bathroom mat.

THE WARP

A thing to be remembered when choosing the warp for a rug is that it should normally be a thinner thread than the weft material. This is because in a rug the warp is usually covered and so not seen. Sometimes, however, the warp is intended to form part of the design, perhaps even a dominant part as in the Warp-Faced Rug, Plate 10; in such cases one can perfectly well use a warp that is thicker than the weft.

For wool rugs, woven or tufted, we generally use the 'linen rug warp' produced by Craftsman's Mark Ltd. This is an excellent twine, very strong, shiny and rather slippery to handle.

Should the warp required be a coloured one, this yarn, which is light fawn, will dye satisfactorily to darker shades. For lighter shades one would have to use a bleached yarn. J. & W. Stuart Ltd. supply a good white cotton fishing twine in various thicknesses.

Occasionally we have also woven wool rugs on 10/6 ply cotton twine used double. This produces a heavy warp which, of course, adds to the weight of the rug and reduces its tendency to slide underfoot on a wooden floor; incidentally it will give more body to the fringe.

For the rug in Plate 1 we used a woollen warp, $4/5\frac{1}{2}$s Grey Wool from the Multiple Fabric Co. Ltd. This is a dark grey yarn which blends suitably with any dark-toned rug. It is reasonably priced and being slightly oiled is pleasant to work. It is best used double in the dents. This firm also makes a $4/5\frac{1}{2}$s camel hair yarn which is slightly softer and paler in tone but extremely strong. Their 4/6s white wool would make an excellent warp for a white or very light-toned rug. We feel, however, that all these yarns should be used double in a 4-to-the-inch dentage.

Our rag rugs are usually made on a warp of 10/6 ply white soft cotton twine from the Linen Thread Co. Ltd. If the rug is intended for a place where it would have to take a great deal of wear, then it might be advisable to use the linen rug warp mentioned earlier, for it is always the warp that has to take the main strain in a rug.

Southwick and Case Ltd., of Liverpool, produce a satisfactory cotton warp twine which is inexpensive, quite hard wearing and will dye well. For extra strength and weight this can be used double. The same firm supply a No. 10 8/5 cotton twine, somewhat thicker than the 10/6 ply for rag rugs, which is suitable for rush matting.

WEFT MATERIALS

Wool is undoubtedly the finest material for rug-making. It is pleasant to handle and wears well. It can be obtained in a great many different thicknesses and colours, and it is easy to dye if a special shade should be required.

Most of the wool rugs made by us and illustrated in this book have been woven from 6-ply Rug Wool or 2-ply Carpet Wool from the Weaver's Shop Ltd., Wilton Royal Carpet Factory, but we have also obtained some excellent 6-ply from Dryad Handicrafts.

Craftsman's Mark stock a good range of medium and fine Welsh Wools in white, off-white and dark natural, as well as Cheviot wools and 2-ply rug yarn in white, all very good quality materials for the hand weaver.

Stoddarts of Halifax supply a strong 6-ply rug wool which is very suitable for the foundation weave in tufted rugs, and also a variety of Axminster 2-ply carpet yarn in thrums. These are rather too short for comfortable handling in a tufted woven rug and are really intended for hooked rugs made on a canvas foundation.

We have referred to 6-ply and 2-ply without so far indicating why one should be used rather than the other. The difference between them is purely a matter of thickness, which however also means speed of working. It is astonishing how quickly one can cover the warp using a 6-ply. On the other hand, the 2-ply is thin enough to be used double and even treble, which means that one can mix the shades to achieve one's tones, blending colours for instance, by even twistings of the strands, or giving emphasis to particular colours in particular places by twisting the strands in such a way as to make a special one predominant at a time. (See Plate 13 for a rug woven by this method.) We have also used 6-ply double (Plate 15), but this produces less interesting results.

A general principle—though by no means a rule—would be to use 6-ply where it is the weave pattern which is the chief feature of the design, and 2-ply where colour and the play of tones is the effect mainly sought. There is of course no reason why both should not be combined in, for instance, a rug of solid colour relieved by a design in blended tones. It is however, important to study the effect that different plys have on the tension of the warp and if necessary, to counteract it by laying in the thinner ply more loosely.

A material not commonly used in this country is hair, but in Scandinavia cow and horsehair in the proportion of two parts hair to one part wool find satisfactory use in rug-making. Naturally hair is not considered to be in the same class as pure wool but it is valued for its exceptionally hard-wearing qualities. It has one drawback for the hand weaver in that its rough, prickly nature is hard on the hands and for this reason is not recommended for anyone who has a sensitive skin.

In Britain the Multiple Fabric Co. Ltd. will supply horsehair as well as some other unusual materials such as human hair reinforced with nylon yarn. This is an unyielding material to work and its total lack of elasticity causes tension troubles which make it difficult to use in conjunction with any other yarn. It is however very durable, and woven on a warp laid in a dentage of 4 to the inch, beats down very well and covers the warp. With a smaller dentage it does not cover so well but will produce a thinner hard-wearing type of rug. (See Plate 1 for an illustration of an experiment in this kind of yarn.)

Rush mats and runners lend themselves to considerable variety both in warp and weft. The warp is usually set up in well spaced-out groups, especially if a fairly coarse material is used such as a thick hemp. For the weft all manner of things can be introduced to relieve the rushes, such as bamboo splits, thick rope and unspun jute. Our example on Plate 14 is a simple one, as it happens, and is woven with Natural Green Rush Plait from Jacob, Young and Westbury Ltd. and natural hemp. The warp is a cotton twine from Southwick & Case Ltd.

Rag rugs form an important class of floor covering, although less so in this country than on the Continent, and particularly in Scandinavia where they are an almost universal feature of the home. Being made of rags they are obviously not of the same quality as wool and will not last as long. But they are extremely interesting to design—and to look at—with all the variety of texture and colour they can offer, and are admirably suited to present day tastes in wall finishes, light coloured wooden floors, and furniture. And if their shorter life be objected to, it must be remembered that this is more than compensated for by their relative cheapness, which makes them fairly easily replaceable.

The weft is composed of rags cut or torn into narrow strips, but this does not mean that one can use any worn-out, beat-up material. On the contrary it must be of good quality with plenty of life left in it: anything less will merely produce a rug that looks shabby and unattractive and will begin to disintegrate in quite a short time. Ideally, of course, one would use new materials in the form of good-sized off-cuts and remnants—so called 'fents'— from cotton mills, shirt and dress factories, etc. Unfortunately most of these already have their regular large-scale customers, so that a source of supply is not easy to find. It is worth studying advertisements in trade papers (such as *World Fair*) and inquiring around in the locality.

For these rugs almost any kind of natural material will serve; cottons, and linens such as sheeting, dress materials, stockinette and corduroy as well as velvet and woollen cloths. Silk can be used, but sparingly for in the weights in which it is obtainable it is rather light. Many of the man-made materials are not very suitable. Nylon, for example, is not bulky enough and plastics are harsh in colour and texture. Terylene and Dacron, now being used as dress fabrics, can be introduced to a limited extent in order to produce some particular decorative effect.

Since the source of the materials is what it is, one cannot expect to have large supplies of any one type available. Fortunately they all mix well and their differing qualities, velvet and cotton, for instance, enable the most interesting varieties of textures and tone to be built up. However care has to be exercised in the weaving itself, as different materials produce different tensions in the warp which have to be taken into account if the finished work is to be perfect. Thus cotton, velvet and especially stockinette must be placed very loosely in the shed, whereas bulkier stuffs such as corduroy and wool

Plate 13 *Wool Rug* (p. 108) *showing Oriental Fringe completed at one end*
Designed and woven by Klares Lewes

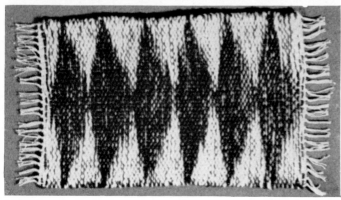

Plate 14 *Rush Mat*
(p. 109)
Designed and woven
by Marlene Frühoff

Plate 15 *Sample Wool*
Rug Weave (p. 108)

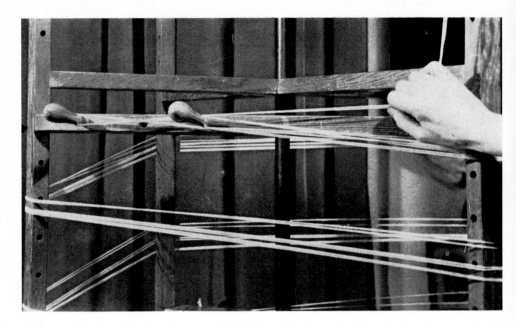

Plate 16 *Making the Parrey Cross*

Plate 17 *Securing the Cross*

require much less slack. It follows that if a mixture of materials is being worked into a rug, the weaving technique must be modified to suit the particular constituent.

CALCULATION OF QUANTITIES

Before embarking on a weave it is well to have available all the material that will be required. It would be annoying, for instance, to run short of a colour and then find that it cannot be matched, a misfortune not unusual, especially when the weaver has dyed his special shade by methods which are, perhaps, slightly irregular.

This means that one must be able to calculate how much will be needed.

In the case of the warp the answer is given by the formula:

$$\frac{\text{Length of warp} \times \text{number of threads}}{\text{Number of yards per lb. Spool}}.$$

In other words multiply the length of the warp in yards by the number of warp threads to be used, and divide by the number of yards in the spool. The result is the number of pounds of yarn required. Unfortunately, although the calculation is easy in itself, it is complicated by the diversity of measures traditional in this country.

All yarns have a yardage per lb. which depends on the weight and thickness of the yarn. The figure which gives this information is known as the *count*.

For cottons it is the number of 'skeins' containing 840 yards which make up one pound. A yarn of 10s count has 10 skeins of 840 yards per pound, which means that 1 pound of 10s cotton contains $840 \times 10 = 8400$ yards.

If the yarn is a ply and not single stranded, the number of skeins of the single yarn is usually given first and the ply number second. Thus 10/6s means that 10 skeins of 840 yards have been used to make 1 pound, but since the yarn is 6-ply the actual yardage will be $\dfrac{840 \times 10}{6} = 1400$ yards.

In linen the figure mostly used is the number of 'cuts' or 'leas' of 300 yards each which make up 1 pound in weight. The calculation is exactly the same as for cotton, save that the figure 300 is substituted for 840.

Unfortunately not all manufacturers reveal their count. The Linen Rug Warp from Craftsman's Mark, for instance, is not marked with a count. It happens to contain approximately 530 yards per lb, and is presumably therefore not based on a standard count. Where the figure is not known it is necessary to ask the supplier for it.

In the case of wools and worsteds, the count is related to the fleece and indicates the number of hanks of 560 yards to the pound. A fleece that will spin a yarn making 40 hanks of 560 yards each to the lb. is termed 40s.

For woollen yarns there are a number of different counts in use in Britain; for example Yorkshire uses the number of 256 yd. hanks per lb.; the west of England the number of 320 yd. snaps per lb.; Galashields the number of 300 yd. cuts in 24 oz. If the particular standard cannot be discovered, it will be necessary to calculate the length of a sample skein by counting the number of threads in the skein and multiplying it by the length of the circumference.

Having calculated the actual yardage required for a warp, a margin of something like 25 per cent will have to be added to allow for a number of factors. For instance, there is a certain amount of 'take-up' of warp over the thickness of the weft, and also some shrinkage in the finished rug after it has been removed from the tension of the loom. There is a measure of waste in the tie-up of the warp on back and front rollers. Lastly there must be an allowance of about 6 inches at each end of the rug to enable fringes to be knotted.

The single formula given at the beginning of this section now seems to be a little more complicated. This, by way of illustration, would be the actual calculation for the warp of a rug 8 ft. long (making a 10 ft. warp with the allowance), 36 in. wide and with a dentage of 12 threads to the inch, using the 10/6 twine:

$$\frac{10 \times 432}{1400} \ (= 36 \times 12),$$

which gives a figure of a little over 3 lb. of warp string.

The weft calculation is very much simpler, not to say rough-and-ready. In fact it depends a great deal upon individual technique, such as the tightness or looseness of one's weaving, so that it is necessary to learn by experience.

As a starting-point for woven rugs, try 2 lb. of wool per square yard for a woollen rug, and 3 lb. of prepared strips per square yard for a rag rug. These quantities should certainly suffice and may be found generous.

For a tufted rug no formula is really practical, since the quantity required depends upon the lengths of the tufts and the closeness of the weave. The best solution is to work a few inches, note the quantity used, and base the calculation upon this.

CHAPTER THREE

Preparing the Loom

PREPARING THE LOOM in readiness for weaving is neither a mysterious nor a particularly difficult operation. But it is a fundamental one upon which the smooth running of all the later work depends. Mistakes made now will be very hard to correct when weaving has actually begun. Consequently it pays to check—and where the beginner is concerned, re-check—every stage.

LAYING THE WARP

The first step is known as 'laying the warp', which means, as the expression implies, the preparation and transfer to the loom of a warp of appropriate length and having the right number of strands for the intended weave.

The appropriate length in this case is not necessarily a length sufficient for one rug. Preparing the loom is quite a lengthy process, and it will pay therefore to arrange one's weaving programme so that a warp can be laid sufficiently long to enable several rugs to be produced. This, too, will save yarn, for there is quite an appreciable amount of waste at the beginning and end of every warp.

Having obtained the necessary quantity of the selected warp string, place two or more cops on the metal rods of the spool rack, arranging them so that the left-hand threads unroll from underneath and the right-hand threads from over the top of the cops (Fig. 7). This will prevent them from tangling later. If you have no spool rack, the cops can be fed out of boxes, or flower pot holes, or any makeshift arrangement which will keep them separate.

The warping mill or warping board must now be set up in a convenient position a few feet away from the spool holder (Plate 9).

There is no fundamental difference between these two pieces of equipment which are, after all, merely a simple means of measuring off desired lengths of yarn. The mill has the greater capacity and is speedier in use; on the other hand it is bulkier and therefore not so convenient to store, and it is also more expensive to buy.

When using a mill the first thing to do is to work out how many times one must wind the string round it in order to achieve the required length of warp. If it has sides, say 3 ft. apart, then once round straight along will produce 12 feet, and if the warp is to be 10 yards long, not forgetting the 25 per cent allowance for wastage already referred to in Chapter 2, then $2\frac{1}{2}$ turns will be required. This calculation is however only an approximation, since the turns will be made diagonally, not straight along, and the exact length of the first turn will therefore have to be measured and divided into the length of warp in order to give the total number of turns required. Having taken the measurement, set the cross-bars in their correct position on the mill, one near the top and the other lower down and insert two pegs in each cross-bar in such a way that the distance between the first peg on the top cross-bar and the last peg on the bottom cross-bar, after having made the calculated number of turns, is the total length of the warp.

The principle of the warping board is similar save that there is a greater number of pegs which will have to be arranged in such a way that taking the string up and down round the pegs will produce the warp length between the first and the last pegs (Fig. 8a and b).

This is the normal arrangement for ordinary rug warps, but if the warp is a very elaborate one, then an additional cross (see below) is made at the beginning which will involve an additional peg. This is the arrangement shewn in Fig. 8a and b, where the pegs are marked A, B, C, and D, E. Plate 16 shows the hole which would take the third peg.

Tie the ends of the threads from the spool rack together (2, 4, 6 or more according to the number of cops being used) and loop them on to the first peg, half the threads over and half under. Then pass all the threads over the second peg and start the mill spinning gently (or make the journey from peg to peg on the warping board) until after the required number of turns you reach the end pegs, where the threads are taken over the first and under the second. The string should be kept reasonably taut, so as to prevent it from sagging, but not so taut as to cause it to stretch.

Now reverse, that is, take the threads round and over the last peg, then under the next one, and spin back to the beginning where this time the threads will go under the second peg and over and round the first one. Thus the threads cross each other between the two pairs of pegs and these crosses are known traditionally as the 'Parrey Cross'—the first one—and the 'Porrey Cross'.

The total width of the warp governs the number of journeys between the crosses, but width shrinkage in weaving must be allowed for by adding 2 inches per yard to the intended width of the rug.

46

Suppose the warp is intended to be 32 inches wide and with a dentage of four threads to the inch, then the number of threads needed is 128. However, the selvedges need extra strength and this is provided by doubling the first and last four threads of the warp, giving an additional eight threads or a total of 136. If you are using four cops, then each complete journey from the first peg to the end peg and back again will lay eight threads and the number of journeys to be made to produce the width of 32 inches will be 136 divided by 8 equals 17, finishing of course at the first peg.

To keep a check on the number of threads actually laid, count them from time to time at the Porrey Cross and mark off into groups of, say, twenty threads. You will probably want both hands free, so tuck the threads you are holding into the already laid warp in such a way that the tension does not slacken. The simplest way of marking is to pass a coloured thread round the first group, leaving the ends hanging ready to be crossed and passed round the next group as it is laid and so on to the end when they can be tied in a knot. The reason for grouping in twenties is that in a dentage of four to the inch, twenty single threads represent five inches of warp. If you prefer you can choose some other group suitable to your dentage, but it is wise to calculate in terms of inches.

When the required width has been laid, cut the threads from the cops at the first peg and knot them round it.

The next step is to secure the two crosses, and this is done by passing a length of coloured string round each and knotting the ends (Plate 17). The strings should be somewhat longer than the total width of the warp, for they will later have to span it and be tied to the shed sticks at each end.

Lastly the end loops must be secured, again by tying a piece of string, which can be quite short, round each (Plate 17).

MULTI-COLOURED WARP

When the warp is intended to show, thus making a contribution to the general effect, it is sometimes made up of two or more colours, either for the purpose of producing a double woven rug, that is to say a reversible rug in which front and back differ, or else for rugs having stripes which run lengthways, or, together with weft stripes, making a plaid rug.

The double warp presents no difficulty. For this two colours are used and they alternate. In laying the warp1 therefore, all that is necessary is to use an even number of spools on the spool rack, half in the one colour and half in the other. Try it with four spools, being careful to place the one colour on the upper rod, the other colour on the lower rod. Knot the ends of the four

47

threads together and lay the warp in the usual way, when you will see that the colours alternate.

If the warp's contribution is intended to be vertical stripes, then the different colours will have to be laid in the appropriate groups and a careful count must be kept of the threads.

Suppose for instance we wish to lay a 20 inch warp to produce an 18 inch runner striped 3 inches grey, 4 inches orange, 6 inches grey, 4 inches orange and 3 inches grey. Since the warp is intended to show, the dentage used will probably be fairly close, say 24 to the inch.

Have spools of both grey and orange on the spool rack, and, starting with the grey wool only, lay 3 inches of warp (i.e. 24 × 3 threads), finishing at the top cross. Break the threads and tie their ends in a firm knot round the first peg, being careful not to allow the warp tension to slacken. Next, starting at the first peg, lay 4 inches of orange (i.e. 24 × 4 threads), finishing off as before at the first peg. Repeat for the 6-inch grey, the 4-inch orange and the 3-inch grey, until the warp is complete.

CHAINING THE WARP

The warp is now laid and ready for 'chaining', a process designed to keep it from getting tangled after it has been taken from the mill or warping board.

For this sleeves will have to be rolled up to the elbows and wrist-watch or jewellery that might catch in the strings removed. If you have been using a mill, you will welcome someone's help in checking its movement, for it is liable to spin out of control, leaving you with a mess of warp round your feet. Alternatively you could block it and walk round while unwinding the warp.

Holding the warp end with the left hand, take out the first peg and slide your right hand through the loop, grasp the warp a little farther along at the second peg and draw a length back through the first loop. This makes a second loop. Insert your right hand into the second loop and repeat the process, continuing until the whole warp has thus been drawn into a series of loops (Plate 18). The process is very like that of crocheting, using your hand instead of a crochet hook, and the result is a 'warp chain' which stays very tidy.

If the mill has normally to be kept stored away, then it is worth laying several warps at a time which can be kept in a drawer until needed. They should of course be labelled with particulars of length and number of warp threads.

'BEAMING ON'

The chained warp can now be transferred to the loom, a step known as 'beaming on'. The loom however must first be made ready to receive it. The heddle shafts are tied together to prevent tangling and either secured to the upper cross-bar or lowered on to the pedals to be out of the way. The reed is removed from the batten beam, and the raddle fastened in its place, either seated in the reed groove or, if this is too narrow, by being tied on with string. Remove the raddle top bar, making sure that the wooden pins which hold it are tied to the frame so that they cannot get lost. The raddle should be centred on the beam and this is easily done if the centre points of raddle and beam are measured off and marked in pencil so that it is only necessary to line up the marks.

When the loom has thus been made ready, take a shed stick and pass it through the end loop of the warp at the Porrey Cross (Plate 19). This stick is then tied at both ends to the *cloth stick* and will be finally fastened all along it when the raddling has been done. To ensure that the warp does not slip off the shed stick we unknot the long string with which we secured the cross and tie each end to holes drilled in the ends of the shed stick. This serves the additional purpose of keeping the cross safe: if it should happen to get lost, the sorting of the threads will be made very difficult and a tangled warp will follow all through the weaving.

RADDLING

The purpose of raddling is to comb and spread the warp so that the threads are sorted into their correct position for rolling on to the warp roller.

The warp must first be centred in the loom, and since the centre is already marked on the raddle, all that needs to be done is to measure off half the warp width (16 inches in the imaginary example we used when laying the warp) on the raddle to the right of the centre mark and mark the appropriate dent. This is where we shall place our first pair of warp threads.

The warp must now be taken from the back of the loom to the front, but before doing this place a folded sheet of newspaper across the open raddle teeth to prevent the warp threads from catching in them (Plate 19). Now unchain the first few feet of warp by pulling on the loops, bring them to the front of the loom and let them rest on the raddle.

The next task is to sort the warp threads into their proper raddle dents and this is by no means difficult, for although the warp may look something of a tangle, the crosses made when it was being laid will ensure orderliness. Pull the unchained length taut and shake it up and down a little (or better still, get the help of a member of the family to do this for you), and you will find that the warp settles itself into groups of threads, known as 'portees', arranged in the order in which they were laid.

Our first dent is already marked, 16 inches from the centre of the raddle; this represents half the warp and therefore has to take half the warp threads, 68 in number (to go back to our example). The warp was laid on the reed basis of four threads to the inch, but a raddle usually has two dents to the inch, so there will be 32 dents to be filled in this half and the threads will have to be doubled in them. You will remember, however, that our warp allowed for a doubling of the first and last four threads to strengthen the selvedge, and this will have to be repeated in the raddle. Consequently the first two raddle dents will have to accept four threads each, and the remainder two. And this is what we do, working straight across from right to left and into the other half of the raddle, moving the folded newspaper along as we go, tautening the warp from time to time to establish the order of the threads, until we reach the end of the warp and the last two dents which, like the first two, will have to take four threads each.

Having completed the raddling we can now replace the raddle top-bar and peg it securely. Then, in readiness for the rolling on, we spread the warp evenly on the back roller stick (which so far is tied to the cloth stick only at its two ends) and finish off by securing the remaining ties to the cloth stick in such a way that back roller stick and cloth stick are about one inch apart and run parallel.

ROLLING ON

Rolling on is merely the operation of rolling the warp on to the back roller, but it has a very important aspect, which is to ensure not only that the warp is rolled on tightly, but that all its threads are under the same even tension. A loosely rolled warp with uneven threads can cause endless trouble later on in the weaving, for it will inevitably produce an uneven weave, tight in places, slack in others.

Rolling on is best done by two persons, or even three for a heavy warp. One stands behind the back roller, and having made sure that the threads are spread evenly on the cloth stick, takes a half turn or so on the ratchet to bring the cloth stick on to the roller. Place a heavy fold of newspaper over this and go on turning until the warp has been rolled on, but pausing every quarter or third of a turn in order to insert a shed stick. This is placed between the roller and the fresh warp as it comes on, and is thus gripped by it and carried round. The purpose of the shed sticks, of which quite a number will be required, is to prevent the upper strings from cutting into the lower layers

Plate 18 *Chaining the Warp*

Plate 19 *Warp secured by Cloth Stick*

Plate 20 *The Warp raddled*

Plate 21 *Reeding*

which, if it happened, would cause uneven tension. If your supply of shed sticks is insufficient for the length of the warp, tightly folded lengths of newspaper can be used in exactly the same way and make a fair substitute.

While you are rolling on, your assistant must stand in front of the loom, as far away from it as space allows, and holding the warp with one hand, strain it as hard as possible against the pull of the roller while combing it constantly through the fingers of the other hand so as to free the threads from entanglement. Again the object must be to keep all the threads evenly tensioned, and so tight that turning the ratchet is for you a real effort; you must run your hand frequently across the warp strings as they approach the back roller to test tension.

Although it is obviously better to have an assistant, rolling on can be done single-handed. Pass the warp over the breast beam, spreading it there as widely as possible, and bring it back under the batten to where you are standing behind the warp roller. You can then grip it tightly with one hand while the other operates the ratchet. You will have to drop it in order to have both hands free to insert the rolling on sticks, but this will not affect the tension of the threads already on the roller.

Rolling on should continue, the warp being gradually unchained, until the second cross, the Porrey Cross, is within about 18 inches from the raddle. Now take the end by its loop, lift the coloured string which marks and secures the cross, and insert a shed stick through the warp on each side of the cross. The sticks are secured and prevented from sliding out of the cross by passing a piece of string across the warp and tying to the ends of the stick, for which purpose holes are drilled there (Fig. 16).

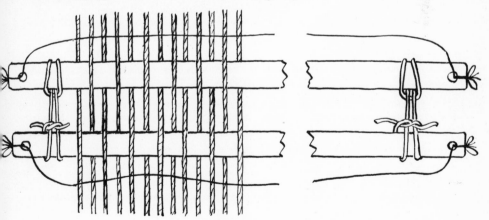

Fig. 16. Securing the Cross

Next remove the string marking the cross and cut through the end loop of the warp, without however, letting go of the end, for if you do the shed sticks will slip out and the cross be lost. The threads should be tied together in little bunches of a dozen or so, using slip-knots which will be easy to undo later. The warp end can now be left hanging against the front of the raddle while you make ready for the next step (Plate 20).

THREADING UP

This, too, can be done single-handed, but someone available to help by passing the threads to you in their correct order for threading through the heddles will speed the job enormously.

Remove the top bar of the raddle and then the raddle itself after having freed the warp, allowing the tied warp ends to hang loose. Take a few more turns on the ratchet so as to bring the two shed sticks fairly close to the back roller, but leaving sufficient length of warp to reach the heddles. It will be as well to tie the shed sticks loosely to the back roller so that they do not slip down during the threading. At this stage tie the two shed sticks together at each end (Fig. 16).

The two castles are now hung from the top beam of the loom and the upper heddle shafts placed in the appropriate grooves (Plate 4). Have the shafts at a convenient height for comfortable working.

Threading up is best done seated in front of the loom. The order of thread-ing is one of the factors which determine the pattern of the weave, and this is fully dealt with in Chapter 5. Here by way of illustration we shall deal with the simplest case of all, a tabby thread-up using only two heddle shafts in which the threads are passed alternately through back and front heddles.

Starting at the right, take the first two threads of the warp and pass them through the first heddle on the back shaft. The next two threads go through the first heddle on the front shaft. Repeat with the second heddles on back and front shafts. These double threads, you will remember, are needed for the selvedges. Thereafter the work proceeds a single thread at a time, but still alternately back and front shafts, until the last two pairs of heddles are reached, when the threads are again doubled for the other selvedge (Plate 5).

The threaded ends are left hanging, but should be tied up in groups, using slip-knots, as you go along. This is of course to prevent them from being pulled out accidentally as the work proceeds.

The proper threading should be carefully checked as you knot each group of threads. A mistake is easily made, especially when you are using four heddle shafts or more, and will be very difficult to correct at a later stage. It will then show itself unmistakably, however, for it will cause a flaw to run the entire length of the weave.

REEDING

When the heddles have been threaded, replace the reed on its batten and centre it as in the case of the raddle, by lining up its centre with the centre mark on the batten. Again, taking our example, measure off 16 inches from the centre and use the appropriate dent as your starting point.

The groups of warp threads are now unknotted, one group at a time, and with the help of the reed hook the threads are drawn through the dents in the reed. They should be threaded in the order in which they were threaded through the heddles, and of course doubled at the selvedges.

Again check regularly for mistakes, and re-knot each group of threads as it is reeded.

THE TIE-UP

The final stage in the dressing of the loom consists entirely of tying up various parts. Hence the name, though as a matter of fact this is often used to denote only one particular aspect, namely the order in which the heddle shafts are tied to the lams and pedals.

Begin by unrolling the cloth on the cloth beam and bring it over the kneebar and under and over the breast beam and lock the roller by its ratchet. Next, unknot the warp strings, one group at a time, and tie them to the front cloth stick in groups of four to eight (depending on the thickness of the string). Several types of knot are suitable for this; the best, however, is the simple reef-knot (Fig. 17a and Plate 6), which should be done as a half tie in the first instance until the whole of the warp has been dealt with.

Each group of threads can now be checked to ensure even tension all along and the knots are then completed. Most workers carry out the process starting at the centre and working outwards so that the selvedge groups are tied last. This makes it easier to achieve even tension all through, and ensures that whatever slight unevenness there may be in the body of the warp, it will not be reflected in the selvedges which will and must be firm.

Next, the heddle shafts which must be tied to the heddle horses or pulleys (Fig. 6).

Fig. 17a.
Reef-Knot

Where only two shafts are being used, one string through each pulley attached direct to one shaft on each side will suffice. If four shafts are used, the strings through the pulleys will go to the centre of each heddle horse (or pulley if pulleys take the place of heddle horses) and further strings from the ends of the heddle horses to the heddle shafts. The actual arrangements are shown in Fig. 18(A).

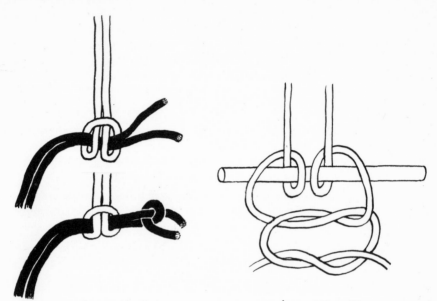

Fig. 17b. *Snitch-Knot*   Fig. 17c. *Warp Tie-up*

The knots used are snitch-knots (Fig. 17b), which are easily loosened to allow for adjustment. Before any adjusting can be done, however, the castles should be removed and this will leave the shafts hanging free. They should now be carefully checked to see that they hang level and at the same height, the height being determined by the centre loops of the heddles which should be in line with the taut warp. The height of the shafts is finally adjusted on the top pulley strings, and it is a help both for this and the other levelling adjustments to tie the upper ends of the heddle shafts together at each end to prevent them rising and falling independently on the pulleys.

The lower heddle shafts can now be tied to the lams and these in turn to the pedals; if the loom has no lams, the shafts are tied direct to the pedals. The normal arrangement with four shafts and lams is to tie the front shaft (No. 4) to the front lam (No. 4), the following one to the corresponding lam and so

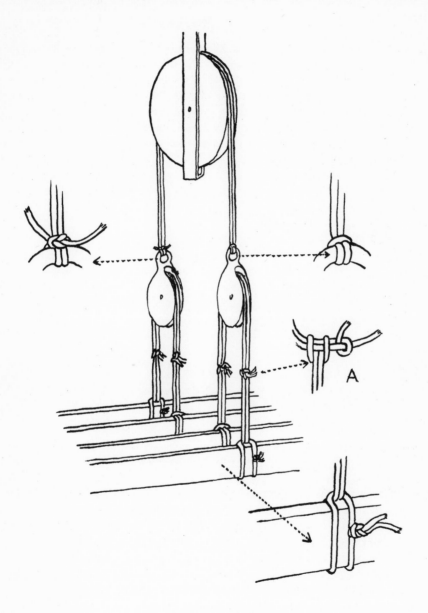

A

Fig. 18. *Tie-up of Shafts*

on (Fig. 6). If only two shafts are in use, then the front shaft is tied to the front lam and the second shaft to the one furthest back.

With four shafts in use, the tie-up to the pedals can be quite complicated and again the reader is referred to Chapter 4 for more detailed explanations.

The tie from shaft to lam, and from lam to pedal is in each case by two separate lengths of cord joined together by a snitch-knot (Fig. 17b). The purpose is to allow of easy adjustment, for the cord is bound to stretch in use and will require checking from time to time. The lams should all hang horizontal, and the pedals should be level and adjusted to a height which is comfortable for working and at the same time gives a good open shed when pressed down.

Finally, remove the cords tying the heddle shafts together, press down the pedals to test your shed, and tighten the warp by means of the cloth roller. You are ready to begin weaving.

POINTS TO REMEMBER

1. If newspaper has to be used because the length of the warp has exhausted the supply of shed sticks, the sheets should be at least six inches wider than the width of the warp, and folded into a minimum of eight thicknesses. Anything less will not serve the purpose, which is to prevent the warp threads from biting into the roll, and so becoming slack. Some more substantial makeshift, dowel sticks, for instance, or odd curtain rods, will obviously be better.

2. Many weavers tie together the shed sticks used to mark the cross. This prevents them from slipping apart during the course of the work. A suitable knot is known in Fig. 16.

3. Mistakes sometimes occur in threading the heddles:
   (a) If a thread has been passed through the wrong heddle, thus spoiling the draft sequence, it is usually best to undo and re-thread from that point onward.
   (b) If the mistake was to pass two threads through the same heddle where there should only have been one, then it is sometimes possible—though not, strictly speaking, advised—to take the extra thread out and wind it several times round the warp roller where it will be out of the way. The warp will then be one thread short in its total width. This will probably not matter, provided the weave is to be in tabby; in pattern weaving it will be disastrous.
   (c) If a heddle has been missed out altogether, pass a new thread the length of the warp through the empty heddle and take it to the back roller

where it can be wound round until it grips firmly and has the tension of the warp. The end can be attached to a bobbin or twist of paper and allowed to swing free. At a later stage steps will have to be taken to secure it to the roller with a knot, or it will slacken and cause a flaw in the weave.

(d) Threads have been known to become crossed. This usually happens between the heddles and the reed, but sometimes the twist is between heddles on different shafts. In any event the threads will have to be unthreaded, straightened and re-threaded. Fortunately the rest of the warp will not be affected.

If the mistake has occurred between heddles and reed, then it is only the threads in the reed that need to be dealt with. If the mistake is between heddles and shafts, both heddles and reed will have to be re-threaded.

(e) For a mistake in reeding, where a dent has been missed out, for instance, or two threads passed through the same dent, the only answer is to re-reed from that point.

However if the rug is a very heavy one, with the warp completely covered by the weft, it is sometimes possible to ignore the mistake because the flaw does not show. This of course should only be done if the mistake was not noticed in time and weaving has already begun.

CHAPTER FOUR

Basic Principles of Weaving. Draft Reading

WE HAVE ALREADY mentioned what is the essence of a weave, namely, the passing of a series of cross threads known as the weft at right angles over and under a series of parallel threads known as the warp. It is friction between the threads which grips and holds them together, and therefore the closer they are forced, the greater the friction and the stronger the weave (though its strength will depend upon other factors as well, principally the strength of the threads themselves).

In crossing our weft threads over and under the warp, we can choose the simple and obvious arrangement, which was no doubt that used when weaving was first invented, and pass the weft over the first warp thread, under the next, over the third, and so on to the end of the row. Alternatively we can choose something a little more elaborate, over the first and under the next two, perhaps, or over two and under two. This will give us a weave having a different structure, or 'weave pattern' as it is called.

Our weave pattern is set up on the loom itself, for what we achieve depends on two factors:

(a) How the warp threads are distributed on the shafts or heddle holders, i.e. the 'thread-up'.

(b) The order in which the warp threads are lowered to form a shed, this depending on the order in which the shafts are connected to the pedals, and the order in which the pedals are operated.

The set-up of the loom which will produce the simplest form of weave, the so-called tabby (Fig. 1), has already been described by way of illustrating the dressing of the loom. The 'over and under' pattern is achieved by dividing the warp equally between two shafts, alternate threads being attached to the first and second, and each shaft being attached to one pedal. These are worked alternately so that first one half of the warp is pulled down, making one weft row, then the other, making the next.

Plate 22 Sample Rag Rug Weave in Twill (p. 110)

Plate 23 Sample Rug in Goose-eye (p. 111)

Plate 24 Sample Rug in Rosepath and Tabby (p. 112)

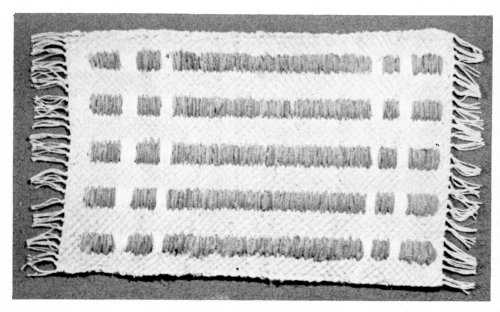

Plate 25 Sample Rag Rug Weave with Spot Pattern (p. 121)

This weave is the basic weave and will produce a flat tapestry surface if the rug is woven in the same wool or other weft material right through. Simple though it may be, however, it still gives scope for an enormous variety of effects. The flat texture of the surface can be broken by introducing thicker or thinner weft materials at intervals. An endless range of colour designs can be produced by variations in the weft colours used. Even the warp can be built up of different colours so that if, for instance, it is laid in stripes and the weft is also woven in stripes of different colours, then a plaid effect will be achieved.

The tabby weave is basic not only because it is the simplest, but also because it results in the greatest degree of friction between threads and is therefore the strongest weave. For this reason it is commonly introduced into other weave patterns which, though attractive, may be structurally weak, in order to give them added strength.

To achieve variety in weave pattern we use different sequences in the over-and-under technique. This is known as pattern-weaving and can only be done by distributing the warp threads on an increased number of shafts, at least four, tied to an increased number of pedals, again at least four, but in rug-weaving preferably six: the additional two pedals can be tied to give a tabby weave which, it will be remembered, often finds a useful place in pattern-weaving in order to strengthen it. It should be mentioned here that a limited amount of pattern-weaving can be done on a 3-shaft loom. This is rarely used and we have not included it, but the interested reader will find useful information on this subject in *Key to Weaving* (see Bibliography).

In pattern-weaving each shaft is commonly tied to at least two pedals, not counting the tabby pedals, but for rug-making anything more complicated should be avoided, for otherwise patterns will be created in which the weft passes over or under four or more warp threads which, having regard to the thickness of the material used, will not look well and will wear badly.

In describing the various weave patterns which are useful to the rug-weaver we shall refer to drafts, and should begin therefore by explaining these.

DRAFT READING

A draft is a diagrammatic analysis of the structure of a weave. It is a kind of pictorial shorthand which tells how the warp is threaded up, how the shafts are tied to the pedals, and the order in which the pedals are worked. In the simplest way possible it tells at a glance all you need to know in order to reproduce any given weave pattern. Let us consider Fig. 19.

Here the spaces between the horizontal lines represent the shafts, No. 1 being that furthest away from the weaver. There are two, and this is therefore a two-shaft arrangement.

The short vertical lines in these spaces represent warp thread. The draft is read from right to left, and we see that the warp threads are alternated between the shafts. Note the two doubles for selvedge (these, however, are frequently not shown, being left to the weaver).

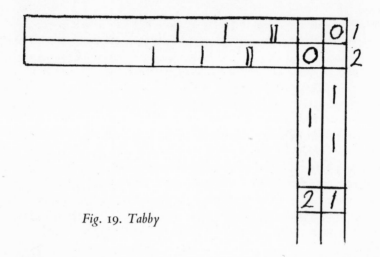

Fig. 19. Tabby

The spaces between the long vertical lines represent pedals, and again there are two. The crossing of horizontal and vertical lines forms squares in two of which dots have been placed. These dots show the tie-up of shaft and pedal, No. 1 shaft to No. 1 pedal, the right-hand pedal, and No. 2 shaft to No. 2 pedal.

The short vertical lines in the pedal spaces indicate the order of pedalling, 1,2,1,2 and so on.

The draft thus indicates a simple tabby weave.

Take another example, Fig. 20.

Here we have four shafts and four pedals. The warp thread-up is the sequence 1, 2, 3, 4; 1, 2, 3, 4, and so on. Each shaft is tied—by way of lams—to two pedals, No. 1 shaft to pedals 1 and 4; No. 2 to pedals 1 and 2; No. 3 to pedals 2 and 3; and No. 4 to pedals 3 and 4. The pedalling sequence is 1, 2, 3, 4, 1, 2, 3, 4.

In this particular example, the draft shows three consecutive series of warp threadings and two pedalling sequences, but this is purely to avoid any possibility of error. For practical purposes it would have been sufficient to show one complete series, which the weaver would then repeat as required by the width of his warp, and the length of his design.

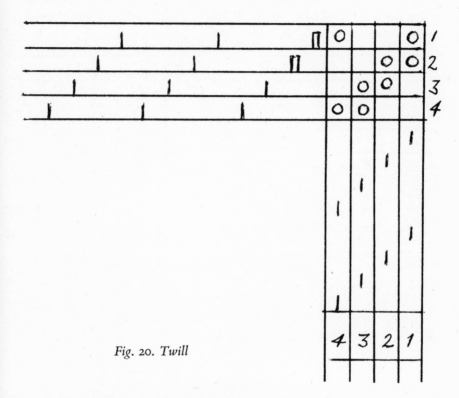

Fig. 20. Twill

A last example, this time showing six pedals, and if you study this you will see that we have merely added two pedals to the previous draft to give us an alternative tabby weave (Fig. 21). We can now, if we wish, vary our weave by doing, say, two 1, 2, 3, 4 sequences, followed by four rows of tabby and repeat. This will produce a completely different texture effect.

The draft method we have described is that most commonly used in this country. There are many others—for instance showing the pedals on the left or numbering the shafts from the bottom up; but they are all based on the same principle and, whether foreign or English, can easily be understood with a little thought.

Before concluding the subject of drafts, it should be mentioned that the weaver can always vary his pedalling sequence. If he does so, he will not, of course, produce the pattern which the draft indicates. He will, however, produce new ones and will find it well worth while to experiment in this direction.

We can now proceed to our pattern weaves, starting with the popular twill.

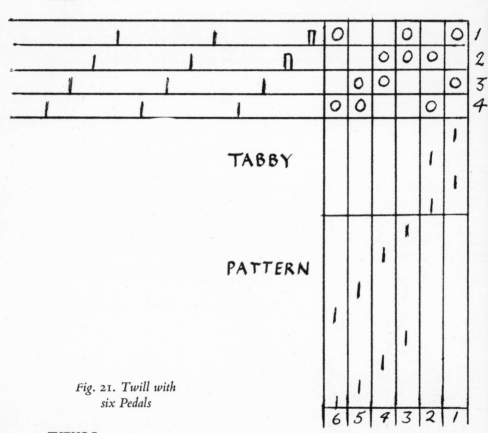

Fig. 21. *Twill with six Pedals*

TWILL

This is in fact the weave illustrated in Fig. 20. Its characteristic feature is the diagonal stripes which appear in the weave, as the appearance of the draft itself in fact suggests.

Twill produces a much thicker weave than tabby, and because of the long diagonals, one which looks glossier and less broken in texture; but because the weft will cover two or three warp threads at a time, it will also be not quite such a firm weave. Plate 22 shows a sample of twill weave; the diagonal striping is plainly visible in the end and centre sections.

Twill was used for linen weaving in biblical times. Another name for it is serge, which was given to woollen cloth woven in twill pattern and used by the Romans some 2000 years ago. The word actually comes from the *sarge*, a kind of cloth square worn by Roman soldiers on the march, and used as a cloak in rain or a blanket at night.

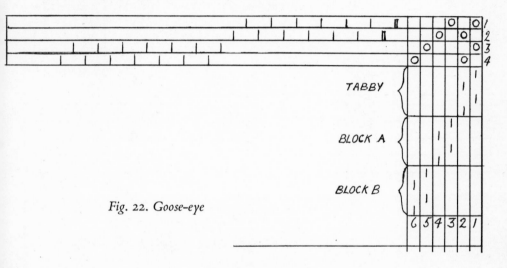

Fig. 22. Goose-eye

There are many variants of twill. A popular one is the 'Goose-eye' with a pleasant diaper-shaped pattern produced by a slight variation in the sequence of the thread-up (Fig. 22; see also Plate 23).

Other variants are produced by changes in the tie-up of shafts to pedals, or in the thread-up or in the pedalling sequences, and a few of these are illustrated in Figs. 23, 24 and 25.

ROSEPATH

This too is a variant of the twill and it can be produced in two forms, one giving a weave with a very definite right and wrong side, the other reversible with a clear pattern on each side.

The latter type is the one we use since it is better suited to rug-weaving. It is also of particular value to the weaver interested in Scandinavian peasant designs, where it is one of the patterns most commonly employed.

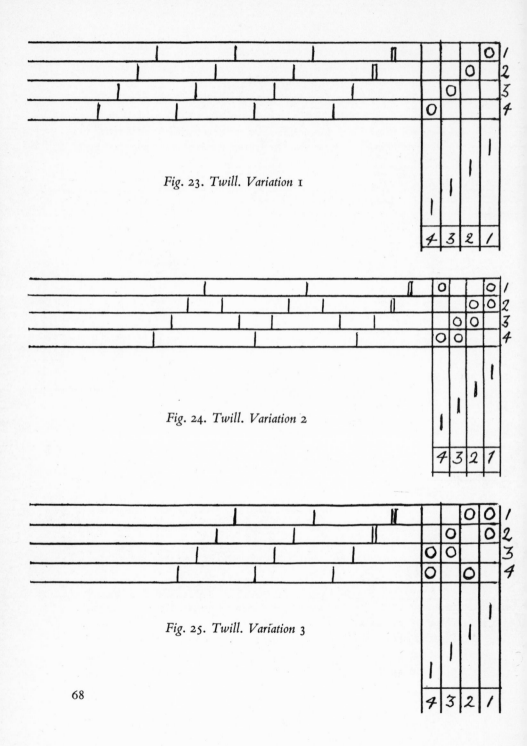

Fig. 23. Twill. Variation 1

Fig. 24. Twill. Variation 2

Fig. 25. Twill. Variation 3

Rosepath is woven on four shafts and with four pedals, but it is one of the less firm weaves which benefits from an addition of tabby. Our draft (Fig. 26) consequently shows the necessary six pedals.

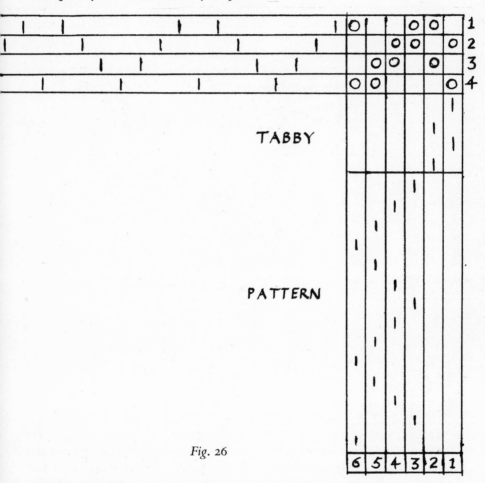

Fig. 26

By varying the pedalling a great number of patterns can be produced; two of these are illustrated in the rugs shown on Plates 24 and 29.

HONEYCOMB

The name of this weave describes its effect. Fig. 27 shows the draft, and a rug will be found illustrated on Plate 26. Like rosepath, it is one of the looser weaves and should therefore be strengthened with tabby. Like the other weave patterns it repays experiment in pedalling sequences, many of which introduce a very happy irregularity to soften the essential geometric rigidity of the pattern.

The weave patterns we have discussed produce their effect by the weave *structure* which they create. Once the thread-up and tie-up have been grasped, any variations are not difficult to understand. Modern tie-ups in fact tend to dissolve the classical ones, seeking to achieve new effects by deliberately re-arranging their regular rhythm.

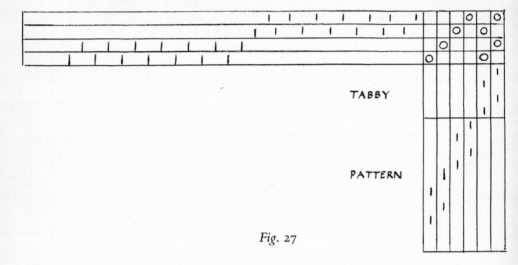

TABBY

PATTERN

Fig. 27

However, the appearance of a rug depends not only upon its structure, but also upon materials and colours and how these are introduced.

Consider the rug on Plate 15. The weave is a simple tabby which, however, does not look quite like that. Its secret is that it is woven with two weft threads (6-ply) on the shuttle, one dark and one light. At each throw the threads have been manipulated in the open shed so as to make either the dark or the light thread the prominent one. The effect is of course automatically reversed on the reverse side.

Alternatively, instead of using only two threads the weaver can take four or five thinner ones, for example 2-ply, in contrasting colour on a variety of tones of one colour; an example is given on Plate 13. The beginner will find it slow work to handle such a number of colours simultaneously, especially since the effect to be achieved will probably have to be worked out

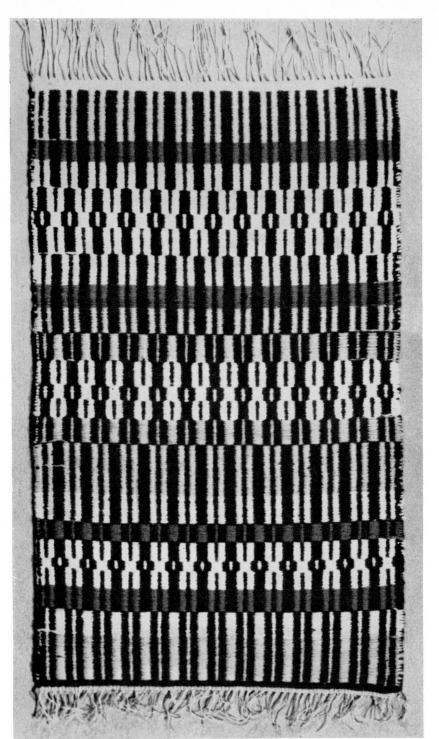

Plate 29 *Wool Rug in Rosepath and Tabby* (*p.* 113)
Designed and woven by Helen Hutton

experimentally; but it is astonishing how practice develops speed and sureness, and what a range of striking results can be produced by this simple method.

A further variation is possible by twisting tightly together several threads of strongly contrasting colours. The twist can be achieved in various ways; either just twist the wools together by hand; or another method which we have found quite useful is to pass one set of threads, say the light ones, through the top of a cone and to wind the dark ones round the outside of it. When winding all the threads on to the shuttle simultaneously from the cone they will be tightly twisted (Fig. 28).

There are various ways of handling this weft. Weaving with the twisted yarn as it comes off the cone produces a jaspe effect. Alternatively sections can be untwisted and the threads placed in the shed in such a way that they lie parallel with each other or alternatively so that one is on top of the other. All three can be used to create variety and interest in a rug and the weaver should experiment. One result of such experiment is shown in our rug, Plate 33. Here in the outer sections the threads have been made to lie one on top of the other in order to produce the zigzag design, while for the foundation the threads have been left twisted. With this method it should be noted that the design is reversed in colour on the reverse side of the rug.

In the middle section the foundation consists still of the twisted threads, but the threads are made to lie parallel in the centre design. Because they are parallel, the appearance will be the same on front and back. It will be seen that the method

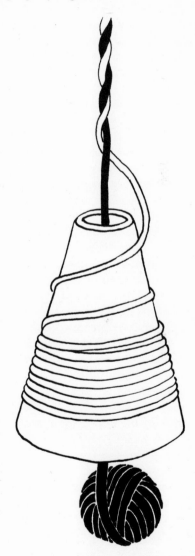

Fig. 28. Twisting Threads

73

produces not only design but also a very marked variation in texture. This variation of texture does not appear in the outer sections, but on the other hand the treatment there used is one capable of producing a much more pronounced design.

Even simpler as a means of introducing variety is to scatter small tufts on the surface, either haphazard or in a regular arrangement. This is done by placing tufts of spun or unspun wool, for instance, or short lengths of rug wool or even rag material, in the open shed in such a way that a part of the material projects above the warp surface (Plate 1). Beating in will hold the tufts securely.

More ambitious, and no more difficult though involving rather more care, are the various ways of introducing pattern by using interlocking techniques. There are three of these, very similar in method, worked on a tabby base and suitable for geometrical angular designs. The first is known as the *Khelim* and is found in Oriental rugs; the other two are the Swedish and Norwegian variants of *Röllakan*.

The essence of the three methods is that in those places in the rug where the pattern occurs the weft is not carried through from selvedge to selvedge in one unbroken thread, but only as far as the edge of the design pattern, and here a fresh shuttle is introduced carrying a different colour to work the actual pattern. This shuttle is passed from pattern edge to pattern edge, when a third shuttle must be used to continue the base weave to the edge of the next pattern, and so on to the end. On the return throw the same shuttles are used, but of course in reverse order. The process is continued until the pattern is complete when the next stretch, which will be plain base weave, will again be worked with one shuttle.

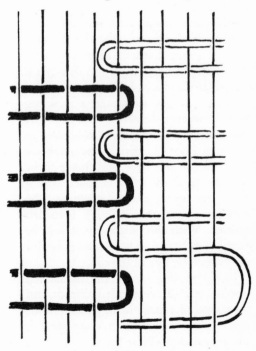

Fig. 29. Khelim Interlock

The difference between the three methods is in the way in which the threads from the various shuttles are locked together, as of course they have to be in order to prevent open splits from forming in the edges of the patterns.

In the Khelim method the problem is solved by wrapping the adjacent weft threads round the same warp thread on the return throw, this causing a slight overlap between them as shown in Fig. 29. (See also Plates 31 and 50.)

In the Swedish type of Röllakan the adjacent weft threads instead of being twisted round a common warp thread, are twisted round each other in every throw (Fig. 30).

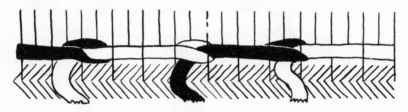

Fig. 30. Swedish Röllakan

In the Norwegian variant the same twisting is employed, but only in alternate rows. This method is the one commonly used nowadays. It is quicker to work than either the Swedish or the Khelim, produces a weave very nearly as strong, and avoids what many people regard as the disadvantage of the Swedish method. In the latter the interlocking produces a ridge on the reverse of the rug along the side edges of the pattern. Using the Norwegian method produces a rug smooth on the reverse and almost of the same appearance as the right side.

The rugs we have so far discussed are all woven in such a manner that the weft is the prominent feature and the warp is practically hidden. There is another technique, however, in which this effect is reversed, so that it is the weft which is completely hidden by the warp, being visible only at the selvedges where the shed is changed from row to row (see Plates 10 and 54).

The 'warp-faced' rug is woven in a tabby weave with a very close dentage and is extremely firm and hard-wearing. The weft may be almost any kind of material, such as rag or thick rope even, so long as it is strong and provides the bulk necessary to bring out the warp in ridges, for which reason this weave is also known as the 'weft rib'. The ridges run across from selvedge to selvedge.

For the warp it is advisable to use something fairly smooth and slippery, since it will be difficult to get a good shed with threads which are inclined to stick together, bearing in mind that they will be used in a thread-up as close as about 24 dents per inch.

DOUBLE-WOVEN RUGS

The reader may perhaps be familiar with some of those magnificent, immensely complicated, hand-woven bedspreads which nowadays are museum-pieces. They were produced in 'double-weave' on looms having as many as 8 or 10 shafts.

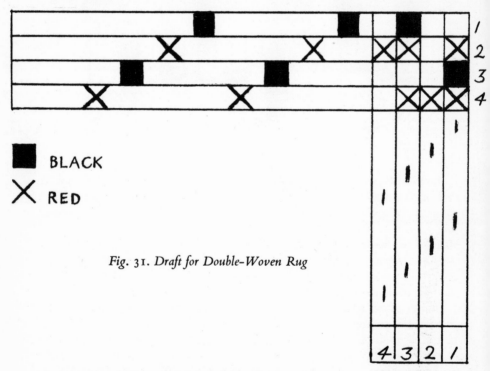

■ BLACK

✕ RED

Fig. 31. Draft for Double-Woven Rug

Rugs fortunately do not require such elaboration and the double-weave technique can be applied in its simple form, using only 4 shafts, to give most interesting effects. It has the additional merit of being a fabric that is extremely strong and hard-wearing.

For a first attempt try a plain-surfaced rug in two colours, say black on one side and red on the other. You will then need a warp laid in those two

Plate 30 *Dining-room Furniture Set designed by Robin Day*

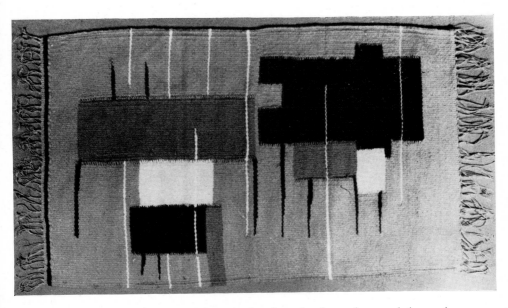

Plate 31 *Khelim type Rug. Design based on the above photograph* (p. 119)
Designed and woven by Helen Hutton

Plate 32 Rag Rug in Tabby and Rosepath (p. 121)
Designed and woven by Klares Lewes

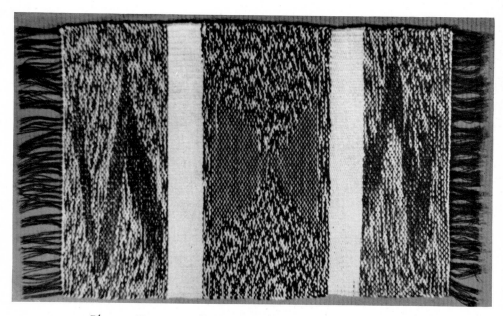

Plate 33 Experimental Rug using three Twist Methods (p. 118)

colours alternately (see page 47), and the threads must be so arranged that each colour is equally distributed between two shafts, black, say on shafts 1 and 3, and red on Nos. 2 and 4.

The weft will need to be in the same two colours, black and red, carried on two shuttles which are thrown alternately and from opposite sides, that is to say one always from the right, the other from the left. It is particularly important that the weft should be put in loosely. Great care must also be taken with the selvedges, bringing the shuttle right round the end warp threads, for otherwise the rug will not hang together.

The tie-up is shown in the draft, Fig. 31, and it will be seen that two of the pedals are tied to three shafts each, and the remaining two pedals to one shaft.

It follows from this arrangement that when the first pedal is pressed, all the red and half the black threads will be pulled down. The black shuttle is passed through this shed and forms the black upper side of the rug. Next the second pedal is pressed, pulling down half the red threads, and the red shuttle is passed through from the left side. This forms the red underside. The process is repeated with pedals 3 and 4.

With four shafts only it is not possible to do pattern weaving in double-weave, but one can achieve blocks of pattern in different colours by using a quite different thread-up and tie-up. These patterns will be reversed on the reverse side. An example is given on Plate 47.

SPOT PATTERN

A very simple way of producing a spot pattern in a weave is to thread a shed stick into the warp in front of the reed by passing it over the threads on which the spots are to be formed and under the remaining threads. If then the stick is lifted, a fresh shed will be created which is quite independent of the shaft thread-up and the pedalling, and which can be used for weaving.

The stick, however, would interfere with the beater. The answer is to lift it and insert another stick into the shed so created, but behind the shafts and as close to the two shed sticks by the warp roller as possible.

The foundation is always in tabby. Start your weave and when you come to a pattern throw, move the stick forward to immediately behind the shafts and turn it on edge. It will stay thus, due to the strain of the warp threads, and form a shed for your pattern throw. Obviously the broader this second stick is, the better the shed it produces.

The pattern throws can be repeated until the pattern has reached the desired size, but each throw should always be followed by a row of tabby. If the repetition is carried sufficiently far, the spots will grow to a lengthways stripe, and this is the result which is illustrated on Plate 25.

79

An obvious development of the technique described is to alter the placing of the stick from time to time in the course of the weave so as to produce staggered rows of dots. The arrangement should of course be worked out beforehand.

POINTS TO REMEMBER

1. At the beginning of a weave when the first few throws of string are put in there is often difficulty in keeping the double selvedge threads flat. The result is a wavy selvedge. To avoid this place four 4 inch nails in the first two throws on each side of the warp, beating them in with the string. They will prevent any tendency to waviness, and can be removed after an inch or so has been woven.

2. Trouble can also be caused by loops of weft forming in or near selvedges. These are usually the result of uneven throwing. If a loop is very small it can usually be eased with the help of a needle in and out between the warp threads until it is completely taken up. Larger loops must be cut and the two cut ends carefully darned into the weave.

3. Beginners' rugs not infrequently show the signs of uneven warp tension in the form of a ruckled surface tightly woven in places and loose in others. The warp should have been carefully tested for slackness during the rolling-on process. Every time you pause to insert a shed stick, check by running your fingers back and forth across the threads and tighten up any that seem looser than the rest. Test again when the rolling-on is complete, and after the threading when you tie the warp to the cloth roller.

But even after these precautions, loose threads sometimes develop during the weaving, and these are much more difficult to correct. They may right themselves after a few inches of weaving and it is worth waiting in the hope that this will indeed happen. If it does not, then the only remedy is to tighten the offending thread by forcing a pencil, or some folded paper or other form of padding underneath it where it passes over the warp roller. Be very careful not to make the padded thread tighter than the remaining warp threads, for this would cause trouble to develop elsewhere.

The padding is really a last resort, for the loose thread will become further stretched by it; this means that the padding will have to be increased from time to time.

4. *A Poor Shed*: Unequal lifting of the shafts or unequal lowering of the pedals will cause a bad shed and make it difficult to throw the shuttle. The usual cause is unequal length of the shaft or pedal cords. They should be carefully checked before weaving begins, but also occasionally during the weaving, for cord stretches in use and sometimes knots slip.

5. *A Broken Heddle*: Cut the broken heddle from the shaft. Untie the top two knots of a new heddle, thread the bottom loop on to the lower shaft and draw it through the loops of the remaining heddles to its proper position. Re-tie the knot of the centre loop round the affected warp thread, and the knot of the upper loop round the upper shaft.

   If the heddle breaks before weaving has begun, it will not be necessary to untie the knot of the middle loop, since the warp thread can itself be untied and re-threaded.

6. *A Broken Warp Thread*: To repair a broken warp thread, slacken off the warp and draw the loose end back on to the weave, re-threading it if it has slipped out of the reed or heddle. Insert a pin in the weave at the site of the break and wind the broken thread round it. Tighten the warp again, making sure that the broken thread has the same tension, and continue weaving. When the rug is finished the broken thread should be darned in.

   If the broken end is too short to reach the pin, lengthen it by joining on a length of thread, and knot it with a reef-knot.

7. *A Wide Carpet*: If two or more runners are being woven for the purpose of being joined lengthways to make a wide carpet, it is important that the pattern shall match across the total width, and quite essential where the pattern consists of stripes.

   The best method to ensure this is to make a template in stiff paper or cardboard by marking on its edge, when the first pattern repeat has been completed, the depth of each stripe or motif change, noting also the colour change. This should be done after the warp has been slackened off. The template should be sufficiently long to allow it to be pinned to the already woven piece.

   As you continue to weave, check the work carefully against the edge of the template, and for your final check of the repeat slacken off the warp again. The slacking off is important because of course the warp is stretched when under tension.

CHAPTER FIVE

Rag Rugs

RAG RUGS DO not seem ever to have been as common in English homes as they
are on the Continent, and particularly in Scandinavia. Perhaps this is because
they are not made of wool, and so were looked down upon as an inferior
article. Since the war, however, they have become steadily more popular,
and deservedly so: for although they are not as hard-wearing as wool rugs,
their cheerful patterns lend themselves wonderfully to modern furniture
and furnishing, and their inexpensiveness more than makes up for their
shorter life.

From the point of view of the weaver interested in his craft, that inexpensiveness has the added advantage of facilitating experiment. He can try out
new designs, weave patterns and colour schemes, and if any particular idea
proves disappointing when translated from sketch to rug—well, he will have
had his trouble, but the cost will be minute.

The trouble, on the other hand, will be rather greater than if he had worked
in wool. This is entirely a matter of preparation. Wool is bought in skeins,
usually of the precise colour needed, which merely need winding into balls
to be ready for use. Rags on the other hand have to be collected, which takes
time, and when collected will be found to consist of all kinds of material in a
wide mixture of colours of which some may be wanted, and others unwanted.

Having collected your rags the first task is to sort them into colours and
sub-grade into kinds of material. When this has been done you will know
precisely what is available, and so can plan the rug in the light of your
resources. Now too is the time to decide whether any of the materials need
to be dyed, either because some shade is not precisely right, or is insufficient
in quantity. And remember always that black and white are invaluable in rag
weaving, for they provide the 'binders' and the contrasts necessary to unify
the multi-coloured stuffs normally collected.

The next step is to cut or tear the material into strips $1-1\frac{1}{2}$ inches wide,
according to thickness. You will soon learn to judge this from experience.
The lighter the material, the wider the strip. Since the rug will be made up
of material of different weights, this is the simplest way to balance them so as

Plate 34 Rag Rug with Inlay Pattern (p. 123)
Designed and woven by Klares Lewes

Plate 35 Rag Rug with Inlay Pattern (p. 125)
Designed and woven by Klares Lewes

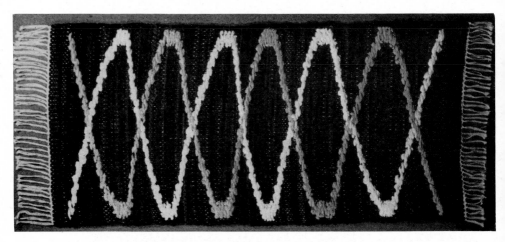

Plate 36 Rug with Inlay Pattern (p. 123)
Designed and woven by Klares Lewes

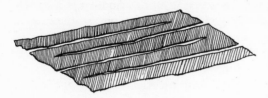

Fig. 32. *Cutting Rags*

to ensure a reasonable evenness of texture.

Sheeting and cotton materials are generally best torn, but most woollens, stockinette and velvet have to be cut. Seams must be unpicked, and any kind of lumpiness cut away.

In order to obtain reasonably long lengths, the strip should be cut or torn to within about one inch from the end of the cloth, then another strip started from that end going back and parallel with the first, continuing until the whole piece has been dealt with (Fig. 32). This will result in one long continuous strip having, however, a number of corners where the edges of the original material occurred. Tidy these by rounding off the 'ears' (Fig. 33). When weaving, these turnings should be given two or three firm twists; they will then be perfectly strong, will lie well in the shed and beat down smoothly.

Prepare a good supply of material, so that the weaving will not be constantly held up by the need to cut fresh strips; roll each colour into handy-sized balls, and place in a basket or tray. Work then will be just as orderly as when weaving wool.

Always begin and finish a rag rug by weaving some half-dozen rows of tabby, using for weft the same string as was used for the warp. The first 2–4 rows of the actual rug, as well as an equal number of the last ones, should also be woven in tabby. This makes good firm ends.

The strips should be carried on a long shuttle, one the width or almost the width of the warp. Make sure that you have a good shed, this being even more important with rag rugs than with wool.

The weaving process itself is exactly the same as when using the more conventional weft materials. Beating however, needs to be more vigorous to ensure a close texture, and the strips should be laid very loosely and wavily in the shed (Fig. 34).

To meet the difficulty caused by the relative shortness of the strips, some weavers sew together all the rags of one colour to form a single long strip. This is a lot of work, however, and

Fig. 33. *Rounding Strips of Rags*

85

moreover restricts you very much when you want to vary texture and tone.

An entirely effective and much more simple method is to use the strips as they come, but when you reach an end turn the last couple of inches round the nearest warp string and pull it back in the opposite direction, without changing the shed. Press down and introduce the new strip, still in the same shed, so as to overlap the old strip and with its beginning twisted round a warp string. Beat hard.

Rag rugs can be woven in tabby or in any of the pattern weaves already described. The rugs we have chosen to illustrate some of the possibilities are in twill (Plate 22) and in a mixture of rosepath and tabby (Plate 32).

One additional technique should be mentioned here, which, though it can be employed perfectly well for other types of rugs, is particularly suited to the rag rug. This is the Swedish *slarvtjäll*, an inlay method of producing a

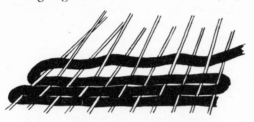

Fig. 34. Loosely laid Weft

design on a flat, mostly tabby surface; it is illustrated on Plates 34, 35 and 36. The material which is to form the design is introduced in the same shed as the ground colour, secured round a warp thread, passed over two or three warp threads of the raised shed, then turned round the next warp thread and brought back in the following shed together with the ground colour. It thus lies on top of the ground colour, which itself is carried straight across in the normal way. The design can be taken up the rug as the weaving proceeds, to make a straight line or a diagonal, changing direction if desired; or it can be used to form short rectangles or triangles or simple blobs.

Instead of taking the design colour over, one can also take it under the chosen warp threads so that it will then be in the same shed as the ground colour. The result will be to soften the strength of the design, for it will be broken by warp threads, and in any case it cannot be made to cover the ground colour completely.

Rag rugs, after being taken off the loom, are finished off with fringes just like other rugs (see Chapter 7). An additional clipping process is necessary, however, for, with the relatively short weft strips normally used, it will be found that both back and front of the rug show numerous little ends of material and frayed threads; these must be cut off with scissors (operated with care so as not to cut any warp threads). There may be a tendency for some fresh ends to work their way to the surface, but this will disappear after a few days.

86

CHAPTER SIX

Tufted Rugs

ENTIRELY DIFFERENT FROM the rugs described in previous chapters are those with a pile surface, the so-called tufted rugs. The tufting may be worked all over, in which case the design of the rug will depend entirely upon the use of colour; or it may be partial in such a way that the areas of tufting themselves form a pattern.

Tufting is always carried out on a woven foundation, usually in tabby; this is necessary in order to give strength to the texture, but in addition it results in a useful economy, tufting being rather greedy of material.

Apart from its use as a foundation, the weave can also be made to serve a decorative purpose. A rug can, for instance, be worked in stripes of tufting alternating with stripes of weave; or small patterns, such as squares and triangles, can be tufted on what is mainly a woven rug (Plates 37 and 38). In these cases, although the tufted portions will still have a tabby foundation, the woven sections in between can be carried out in a pattern weave.

There are several methods of tufting to be described. They have one technical point of great importance in common, which is that the tufting must never be carried out on the selvedge threads. To ensure firmness these are always woven, using a separate shuttle but the same kind of wool as for the tufting. The throws must be double in a kind of figure-of-eight technique, to enable the selvedge to keep up with the bulk of the tufting and give it equal body with the rest of the rug. And every second throw must be interlocked with the tabby foundation of the body of the rug (Fig. 35).

If only a small pattern of tufting is worked on a mainly woven rug, the figure-of-eight weaving does not, of course, arise; but the bulk formed by the tufted rows must still be compensated for by an increase in the number of rows of weave.

The thickness of the tufted, as compared with that of the woven, portions causes a further difficulty which it is important to guard against. It will be appreciated that as the finished work is rolled on to the cloth roller, the tufted sections, especially those towards the centre of the rug, will build up much more quickly than the woven sections. If this is not compensated for, there will gradually develop an unevenness in the warp tension which will be ruinous to the work. Accordingly the woven sections, at least the selvedges in a rug tufted all over, should be padded out on the cloth roller with folds of newspaper, starting as soon as the rug begins to go round the roller and continuing every half-turn or so. The pads should not be placed directly above each other in the early layers of the roll, and of course they should add evenly to the thickness on both edges of the rug. The warp itself should be checked from time to time for evenness of tension by running a finger across the threads at the back roller.

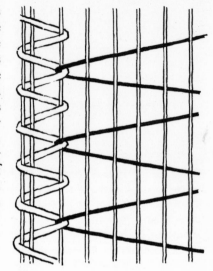

Fig. 35. Selvedge treatment in Part-tufted Rug

CUT LENGTH METHOD

This process consists in knotting short lengths of wool yarn into the warp, each length round two warp threads, leaving the ends of the yarn to project on the surface and so to form the pile.

To ensure an even surface pile, the tufts should all be cut to a uniform length and this is best done by means of a gauge.

The wool gauge (Fig. 13) consists of a strip of wood of convenient length and with one edge grooved. The yarn is wound closely round this and a pair of scissors slid into the groove, or a razor-blade drawn along it, will then automatically cut the wool into equal lengths. If no grooved gauge is available, then any handy piece of wood, such as a flat ruler will serve almost as well, the scissors being inserted through the looped wool when cutting. However, this makeshift is a little hard on the fingers if a lot of wool has to be cut.

The length of the tufts will depend upon the width of the gauge, and it is as well, therefore, to have several gauges of different widths available. When selecting one for a particular rug, remember to make due allowance for the take-up of the knot: a $1\frac{1}{4}$ inch gauge, for instance, will not give finished tufts more than approximately 1 inch long.

Knotting is a simple process. Place a cut length of yarn over two warp threads, bring the ends round underneath and up again between the two threads, and give a sharp tug to tighten. This makes the *Turkish* or *Ghiordes*

Plate 37 *Tapestry and Tufted Rug* (*p.* 127)
Designed and woven by Ronald Grierson

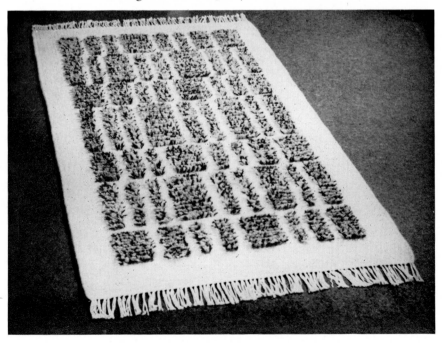

Plate 38 *Tapestry and Tufted Rug* (*p.* 127)
Designed and woven by Ronald Grierson

Plate 39 Rya *Rug* (*p.* 127)
Designed and woven by Anne Meurling

knot, which takes its name from a famous weaving centre in Asia Minor (Fig. 36).

Other knots are the *Soumak Stitch* and the *Chain Stitch*. Neither of these is used in the rugs described in this book, and we would refer the reader who wishes to try them to Ronald Grierson's book *Woven Rugs* (see Bibliography).

As we mentioned earlier, tufting is carried out on a woven foundation, usually tabby, and this foundation is woven at the same time as the tufting is carried out. Begin (and finish) the rug with several rows of tabby to provide a firm end. The next step depends upon whether you wish to tuft in an open shed, which seems to be customary in this country, or in a closed shed, which many Continental weavers prefer.

For the former, change the shed and work a row of knots, the usual two warp threads at a time but they will be alternate threads by reason of the open shed. Now with a shuttle of the yarn you are using as a base (which need not be the same as the tufts) throw a row of tabby, then change the shed and start tufting the second row; you will note that you are now working on the threads which make up the other half of the warp. Finish off with a throw of tabby, change the shed and continue.

Tufting in a closed shed involves knotting all the warp threads instead of only half in each row; the tufts are made as before, but there will be twice as many in each row and they will be much closer together. Nevertheless this is a quicker and more economical method since, because of the closeness of the tufts, it is generally possible to work four or more rows of tabby between each row of tufting. With the open shed method, on the other hand, it will be necessary to work at least three or four rows of tufting to four or five rows of tabby for a good appearance.

Fig. 36.
Turkish Knot

SHORT PILE METHOD

The technique described above necessarily produces tufts that are relatively long, since the lengths of yarn used must be sufficient to enable them to be knotted. A short pile can, however, be produced by a method which dispenses with the use of cut lengths. A gauge will still be needed, however, which can be a pencil, for instance, or a thick knitting needle, or for longer pile a ruler.

Wind the wool into a 'dolly' and pass it down between the two first warp threads (not the selvedge threads), leaving a short end projecting on the top surface. Bring the dolly round the back of the left warp thread and up to the top of the warp again, then across the front of the two warp threads, round the right hand thread, and back to the top passing between the two warp threads and below the loop already made between them. Now place the gauge on the warp where the loops are being formed, take the wool from below over the top of the gauge and down between the next pair of warp threads (Fig. 37). Continue to the end of the row.

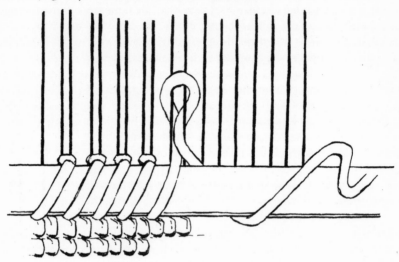

Fig. 37. Short Pile Method of Tufting

If the gauge is shorter than the width of the warp, it can be moved along as the work proceeds. When the row is completed, remove the gauge and weave a foundation row of tabby, beating down well. The knots are now secure and the loops can be cut, or, if a looped pile is preferred, left uncut.

The short pile method is extremely useful for plain surfaces and simple effects generally. Where, however, something more elaborate is wanted, a pattern of blocks of colour perhaps, then it is better to tuft by the first method.

Moreover, the long pile method lends itself very well to the blending of colours: the tufts can be made up of three or more strands of wool (particularly if a 2-ply is used), which gives the weaver a chance to create different tones by judicious mixing and thereby achieve a surface with a lively appearance. The thread in the short pile method can of course be made up of strands of different colours, but there is no possibility of varying these from tuft to tuft.

RYA AND FLOSSA RUGS

These are the Scandinavian versions of the tufted rug and they present a very characteristic and attractive appearance. The techniques used are in fact the same as those customarily used in England and already described, and the differences flow from differences in treatment.

Rya rugs have long, rather shaggy tufts, knotted by the cut length method. The number of foundation rows between tufting varies considerably; one finds as many as eight or ten and (Plate 39) even eighteen rows of tabby foundation between sections of tufting.

Although the foundation is usually tabby, twill is quite frequently used (Plate 40). Moreover the foundation weave is often in a yarn of cheaper but tougher quality than the tufting, particularly if the tufts are sufficiently long to cover and conceal the foundation. Thus one may find horsehair, cowhair, and even rag used.

Rya is very popular with contemporary rug designers who favour tufts that may be as much as 4 inches and more in length. Three good examples will be found on Plates 12, 41 and 51. Many of these modern *Ryas* are so decorative in design and exciting in colour that they have found a place as wall hangings, and indeed there is a tendency to design them specifically for this purpose.

Flossa rugs are very short pile rugs with a much greater density of tufting than in *Rya*. A closer dentage is used for the warp, and fewer foundation rows are worked between the tufting. The tufting is done by the normal short pile method, using a narrow gauge.

IMITATION FLOSSA OR OVERSHOT PATTERN

This is perhaps the right chapter in which to describe the imitation *Flossa* rug, for although this involves no handtufting whatsoever and its technique is that of draft weaving, nevertheless in appearance it is a tufted rug.

The American term 'overshot' expresses very clearly the surface patterning which is that of a long weft yarn, superimposed upon and practically covering a closely woven tabby foundation. These long 'overshot' threads which are formed by the tie-up and the pedalling, are later cut and form a good pile surface.

In a true *Flossa* the pile thread goes across the rug; in the imitation type the pile lies lengthwise of the rug. Imitation *Flossa* is woven on a four shaft loom whereas *Rya* and *Flossa*, when having only a tabby foundation, can be woven on a two shaft loom or a strong rug frame (Plate 3, Fig. 4).

The practical advantage of the imitation *Flossa* over true tufting, which is the relative speed of working, is somewhat offset by the fact that its wearing qualities are not nearly as good. In Finland, the country of its origin, imitation *Flossa* was intended for woven bedspreads or sleigh-blankets, using the tufted side on the inside for additional warmth. The back which was thus on show, was worked with great care and artistry.

A sample imitation *Flossa* is illustrated on Plate 42. The draft, Fig. 54, shows the tie-up, threading and pedalling. Two shuttles are used, one to carry the finer tabby foundation yarn, the 'binder', and the other the considerably thicker pattern yarn for the 'tufts'.

In overshot weaving, the tabby throws alternate with the overshot pattern rows which form the loops in accordance with the tie-up and the pedalling sequence. It will be seen that the warp is so arranged that the threads which form the pile are carried across the top of the weave, passing a set number of warp threads at regular intervals. The pattern yarn, which should be of good heavy quality, must be laid loosely in the shed, in even waves repeated as nearly as possible all through the rug. The foundation web should be well beaten.

As will be seen by studying the draft (Fig. 54), the depth of the pile is controlled by the number of 2,1's threaded in sequence in the B,C unit of the draft.

To cut the pile, remove the rug from the loom, slide a long smooth lath under the overshot threads, and cut across the threads with a razor-blade (Plate 42, which shows half the threads left un-cut to illustrate the 'before' and 'after'). The purpose of the lath is to prevent any accidental cutting of the warp. One end should be sharpened to a point to facilitate entry.

CHAPTER SEVEN

Finishing Off

WHEN THE RUG is complete (remember that the last few rows should have been in plain weave!), the next step is to take it off the loom. If it happens to be the last one so far as that particular warp is concerned, then there is no need for any special care. Simply cut through the warp some 6–8 inches from the end of the rug.

If there is sufficient warp left on the loom to provide another rug, proceed as follows:

Roll the rug well forward over the breast beam, then move the shed sticks which mark the cross right back to the warp beam or roller. It is important to do this because otherwise there is a great risk, when the warp is cut, that the weight of the shed sticks will pull the cut ends of the warp back through the reed and heddles, and the shed sticks themselves will then fall out. This can happen in a flash and will leave you with the tiresome job of re-making the cross and re-threading all the threads.

As a further precaution against any such mishap, start cutting the warp in the centre (again some 6–8 inches from the end of the rug) and work towards the edges. Cut a small handful of threads at a time and tie these together in a knot in front of the reed. This makes sure that the warp will remain secure.

When this has been done the rug can be taken from the cloth roller and the excess length of warp thread on its other end trimmed off, again leaving 6–8 inches on the rug. These threads will be needed to make a fringe.

The simplest fringe to make is the plain knotted fringe. Bring together 2–6 warp threads (according to the thickness of the thread used), tie a loose knot and push this up to the edge of the rug, pressing the end weave well together, then tighten with a firm pull. Continue until all the threads have been knotted and the fringe is complete. Should it appear too long, or is uneven, it can then be trimmed.

The ends of the threads will tend to fray in use, and this is normally accepted. You can, however, prevent it if you wish by adding a second knot at the end of each tuft.

An alternative elaboration is to add two or three more rows of knots so as to form a kind of netting. This is done by taking the tufts formed after the first row of knotting, dividing them in half, and knotting each half to its neighbour in the next tuft, these knots coming about an inch below the first knots. Repeat until you have the desired number of rows. At least 6 inches of warp thread will be required for these knots.

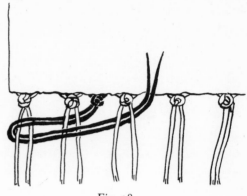

Fig. 38

Woollen rugs are often finished off Oriental-style, with a plait and twisted fringe. This method, incidentally, is not suitable for a cotton twine warp, but only where a stout linen warp has been used.

The cut ends need to be fairly long for comfortable working, not less than 8 inches. Begin by tying all the warp ends together two-and-two as in the method first described. They will be referred to as 'pairs'.

Starting from the left, using a thick needle pass a length of warp thread through the end of the weave and knot the ends so as to form an additional pair between the existing second and third pairs. This gives more body to the edge and will prevent the plaiting from sloping inward.

Take the additional pair and pass it to the left, under the second pair, over and under the first pair and back, over the second pair and under the third pair (Fig. 38). The threads are pressed up as tightly as possible against the edge of the rug, and their ends brought out between the third and fourth pairs.

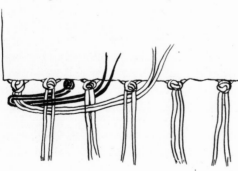

Fig. 39

Now, holding the first four pairs in your left hand, pass the first of these pairs to the right under the second pair, over the third, under the fourth, and bring it out between the fourth and fifth pairs (Fig. 39).

Repeat with the next lot of four pairs until the whole fringe has been dealt with, save for the last three pairs,

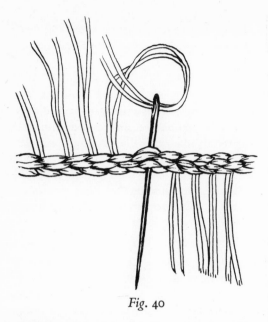

Fig. 40

which obviously cannot be treated in the same way and must be made to disappear by being threaded into the plaiting.

The method described produces a three row plaiting. If greater width is desired, then each pair must be made to pass over and under a greater number of pairs, five, seven or more.

We are now left with our plaiting and all the thread ends on the rug at the top. Starting this time at the right-hand, thread each pair through a carpet-needle and work it down through the plaiting, not however in the same place where it came up, but one space to the right (Fig. 40).

When all the threads have been brought down, thread an additional pair into the left-hand so as to balance the right-hand edge.

To finish off the fringe: starting at the left, take the first pair between the fingers of your left hand, the second pair between the fingers of your right hand and twist each pair to the left. At the same time place the left pair over the right pair and twist the two round each other (Fig. 41). Knot the ends, and continue until the fringe is complete. It should be approximately 3 inches long, and to ensure that all the twists are of equal length, make a paper gauge and measure them as you go along.

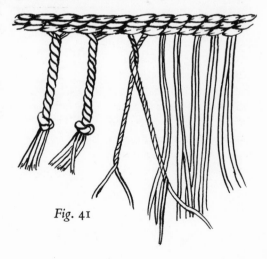

Fig. 41

If no fringe at all is desired, finish off the rug with a hem by weaving 1 or 2 inches of plain weave, using warp thread as weft; then roll into a tight hem.

POINTS TO REMEMBER

1. Much warp is necessarily wasted when a rug is taken from the loom. Try, therefore, to plan a programme of several rugs, lay the warp accordingly, do not take off a completed rug until you have at least two on the cloth roller, when the first one can be removed leaving the second to provide a warp 'extension'. When moving on from the completed rug, roll it to just beyond the breast beam, then while it is still under tension, raise the tabby shed and insert a shed stick, following up with another shed stick in the next shed for firmness. Allow about 1 foot to 15 inches of warp before putting in the edging string which starts the second rug; this will leave sufficient warp between rugs for making the fringes.

2. To join together runners woven with this end in view, in order to enable a wider rug to be made up than can be worked on the width of the loom, lay them alongside each other on the floor and pin together with safety pins at intervals of six inches or so along the entire length. The stripes or pattern should be matched exactly.

With a curved carpet needle and a length of the warp thread used in the rugs sew into the loops formed by the weft on the selvedges, working alternatively from left to right and back again (Fig. 42). Keep an even tension on the thread and make sure that the two sides lie quite flat against each other and that the matching designs do not become displaced.

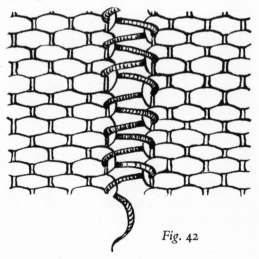

Fig. 42

Plate 40 Tufted Rug (*p.* 128)
Designed by Marienne Straub

Plate 41 Tufted Rug (*p.* 128)
Designed by Mary Patten

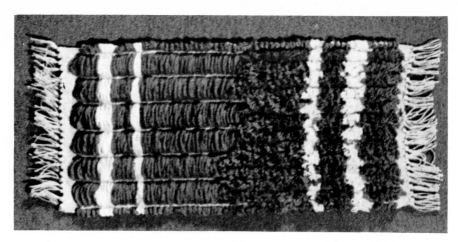

Plate 42 Sample Weave in imitation Flossa *(showing cut section)* (p. 131)

Plate 43 Rya *Rug* (p. 131)
Designed and woven by Brian Knight

CHAPTER EIGHT

Design

THERE ARE CERTAIN basic principles that apply to all forms of design; and of course rugs, if they are to be interesting and successful, must conform to these principles in some degree.

One may have definite ideas about colour, and even strong preferences, but colour alone cannot be relied upon to produce attractive work. The colour or colours must be related to a satisfactory pattern and the tones of colour must bring out the pattern in a well-balanced way. The texture of the surface has a marked effect on the colour and the pattern and the proportion of the motifs in the pattern can have a considerable effect on the suitability of the whole rug for any particular room.

So it is clear that there are several separate factors which have to be considered and reconciled when approaching the problem of design of any type. It is perhaps worth while to take these factors separately and try to give some basic principles which will help the weaver to avoid the main pitfalls in design, though it must be remembered that a master designer will break through the limitations of any rules and produce vivid and satisfying results. But mastery such as this only results from genius or long experience.

Colour is perhaps the most difficult factor to give any rules for because there are so many different preferences and personal tastes to be considered. One has first of all to make up one's mind whether the effect to be arrived at is a warm or a cool one. Then there is the question whether a strongly coloured rug which might look well as the centre of interest in, say, a hall, would live easily with the rest of the furniture in a living-room or a bedroom.

On the other hand, we in England tend to suffer from a lack of adventure in colour; brilliance when well controlled and related can be exciting.

If colours are grouped in the order that they occur in the spectrum they will usually produce a rainbow effect which is unlikely to be happy in a rug. If they are arranged radially, as in a Union Jack, they will again have small hope of success.

Tone, i.e. the intensity of a colour, is of great importance and it is most valuable to try and develop a sense in this direction.

One of the simplest ways of creating interest in a design is by contrasting different tones of one and the same colour. A rug worked out in a series of tones of reds from quite pale pinks through all the stages until a mauve shade is reached could be very successful if controlled with sensitivity. This method usually creates a sense of depth of colour rather than brightness.

Brilliantly contrasting colours are difficult to handle and will usually benefit by the introduction of a neutral colour. Neutrals are the indefinable shades such as warm and cold greys. Khaki is also a neutral colour; it was designed to merge with most backgrounds, as was olive green when used for American battle dress, and both these are very useful as harmonising colours which will relate opposites very successfully.

Contrasts of tones are much easier to use and are indeed very necessary in patterns based on stripes. It is perhaps just as well to warn that over-strong contrast in rugs can bring them into line with linoleum—an effect that nobody is likely to want.

Insufficient contrast of tone very often leads to an indecisive quality which is unfortunately all too prevalent in the weaving design of today. If, for example, one were to lay strips of beige, pale pink, cream and pale green alongside each other the resultant effect, considered as the basis of a rug, could hardly be successful except in the hands of an experienced designer.

But it is quite possible that even a very small amount of black and white introduced as contrasts would bind them into an alive unity.

It has been said with some truth that any colour can be put against any other colour at all, provided that the right tones of such colours are selected and the correct balance of quantities is used.

But in the early stages it is much better to keep to colour combinations that one knows will work and feels will be suitable for the surroundings contemplated for the rug.

Texture is the degree of roughness or smoothness of the surface created by the weaving and the nature of the material woven. Many a design or colour scheme which will not please in a smooth texture can be very attractive in a rough one and vice versa. Very fine results are obtained just by varying the texture of a rug which is woven in one colour alone.

Texture can give pattern and at the same time destroy a carefully planned pattern. A particular colour in a smooth texture will change considerably when used with a very rough surface as the hollows contain a great deal of shadow which mixes with the general colour, darkening it, sometimes cooling it down, but nearly always enriching it: it may then no longer go well with the surroundings for which it was intended and with which, in a smooth texture, it would have blended perfectly.

A heavily tufted rug is particularly susceptible to the influence of shadow and the one reproduced on Plate 44 is a good example of it. Incidentally, it also illustrates the principle of using a series of varying tones of the same colour, as it was woven in deep pinks, warm reds and purples.

Another example of how a colour change can be brought about is when a warp is so closely dented that the weft cannot be beaten down sufficiently to cover it and the colour is then diluted with the warp colour. If this happens to be a white string the change might be quite disastrous. The effect obtained will only be a shade of its original self.

Pattern is a matter very much related to the associations of tradition, no doubt because it is reasonably easy to copy old patterns and translate them into other colours or arrangements, but to invent new ones needs an observant and active eye and mind. Nevertheless new patterns are continually emerging from the hands of the designers of today and finding their way into textiles.

All sorts of everyday surroundings such as pavement pattern, flint walls, telegraph wires, even arrangements of advertisements in the popular press, suggest patterns that can be used in a re-arrangement to start an idea for a rug.

The value of repetition is often overlooked, yet it should be realised that almost any motif if repeated at regular or indeed irregular intervals may look interesting as pattern even though it is comparatively unimportant seen alone.

Man-made forms often lend themselves directly to such patterns, but natural forms almost never do and need formalisation and arrangement before they can be used.

Plates 26 and 27, 31 and 49 give some examples of rugs inspired by such things as a rough stone wall, a pavement, and a furniture display, but there is endless inspiration to be found in many out-of-the-way things. A design does not have to be traditional.

Plates 44 and 45 provide an interesting example of how a design can evolve in an unexpected way. The photograph of volcanic rocky pools was the starting point. The designer felt that its rather exciting tortuous forms could be used to establish the basis of a loosely tufted rug. Several arrangements of this pattern were tried out, but none was quite satisfactory and all seemed to want something of the more definite shape of the light patch in the centre which is suggestive of a narrow triangle with one corner cut off. This shape became dominant in the sketch to such an extent that the designer decided eventually to use it alone as the basis of a repetitive pattern, with the result that is shown on Plate 44.

We have discussed colour, texture and pattern: but it is as well to bear in mind that in a rug these are imposed upon a particular structure, for weaving is always the result of lines crossing each other at right angles. Rugs which respect this structure and incorporate it as the basis of their design will be the most likely to succeed. To go against this principle is to skate upon thin ice and needs experience and practice.

So much for theory. How now are one's ideas to be worked out in practice? Probably the most difficult way is to paint a design on paper, and this is certainly so if one is not experienced in handling brush and paints and in visualising shapes and scale. A much more practical method is to take a sheet of paper of the same proportions as the proposed rug (but of course on a smaller scale) and colour it in the ground colour intended to be used. Then colour and cut out several small shapes in paper and spread them about in various arrangements over the ground colour until an interesting result is discovered. Looking at this design through half-closed eyes often helps one to visualise the final result more definitely. The colouring can be done with water colour, poster colour, chalks or pastels. Oil paint is not advised for designing.

For your ground paper you can, if you wish, use squared paper such as is generally used by designers whose work is to be reproduced by machine; but this is hardly necessary for those who are going to weave their own designs, and it tends to produce a mechanical effect.

Another method is to build up a range of coloured materials of various textures and try out different arrangements of these in stripes or massed groups until you have found a group that will go well together and look right on a floor. This method, incidentally, is very useful either as a preliminary to the previous one or to test its results. For the colour effects one gets down on paper can never be quite the same as those produced by materials, and should therefore always be checked against the actual wefts to be used. When doing this do not simply put together a few wisps of thread: they will not react upon each other in the same way as the solid blocks of colour to be found in a rug, so use fairly substantial quantities.

Another way is to transpose some traditional designs, re-arranging the motifs and colours until a new idea is produced and gradually takes shape as a new design. Simply to copy old designs gives no opportunities to the creative instinct and no chance to experience the satisfaction of having produced something of one's own. Few people are born with a sense of design and a natural sense of colour. But most people can cultivate one or other of these faculties to some degree if they will take the trouble to look around and study good examples with some care.

Plate 44 Tufted Rug (p. 133 and jacket)
Designed and woven by Klares Lewes

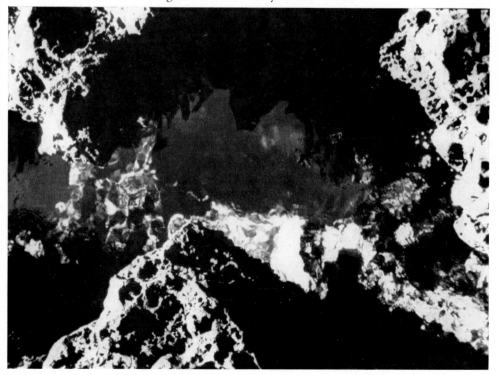

Plate 45 Volcanic Pool—the inspiration for the above design

Plate 46 Rug in Double Weave
Designed and woven by Peter Collingwood

CHAPTER NINE

Plate 11 Tufted Hemp Rug

Designed and woven by Rodney Moorhouse, Des. R.C.A., F.R.S.A.

This rug uses a very novel material, the tufting being of ordinary plumbers' hemp. This was home-dyed to produce a great range of greys, at their darkest a near-black. In addition several neutrals were achieved by bleaching.
  Size: 4 ft. 6 in. × 6 ft. 3 in.
  Warp: Dryad Warp String.
  Dentage: 2 ends to the inch, threaded double.
  Weft: Ground in 6-ply rug wool, home-dyed black. Tufting in plumbers' hemp. Lengths of tufts: approximately 6 in.
  Draft: Tabby.

Plate 10 Sample Warp-faced Weave

  Warp: Wilton's 2-ply carpet wool, grey and orange.
  Dentage: 12 ends to the inch, threaded double.
  Weft: Soft black strips of rag.
  Weave: Tabby.
  Begin and finish off with 5 rows of carpet wool, used single. The weft is only visible at edges. For a description of the weave, see pages 37, 75.

Plate 1 Part-tufted Rug

Designed and woven by Helen Hutton.

This rug is unusual in that the ground weave is in a human hair and nylon yarn. The triangular tufts are in a sage green rug wool, the remaining tufts in natural, unspun washed fleece collected from hedgerows.

Size: 4 ft. × 2 ft. 6 in.

Warp: 4/5½s grey wool (Multiple Fabric Co. Ltd.).

Dentage: 4 ends to the inch, threaded double.

Weft: Ground weave, human hair and nylon mixture (Multiple Fabric Co. Ltd.) approximately 2½ lb. (this yarn comes in 'cheeses' of about 3½ lb.).

Draft: Tabby.

The spacing of the tufts was purposely kept somewhat irregular. The green triangles are made up of 1 inch tufts, with the wool used double, starting with four tufts in the base row, reducing to three in the next row, then two, with a single tuft in the following six rows. The fleece tufts, being of unspun wool, could not be knotted in the same method and were twisted loosely round a weft thread in the open shed and well beaten in with this.

Plate 13   Wool Rug

Designed and woven by Klares Lewes.

This rug, in three tones of orange, two of purple, one of pale lilac and three of deep red, was worked by using five or six different colours mixed on one shuttle and manipulating them in the open shed to create a pattern (pp. 39, 70).

Warp: Rug Linen Warp (Craftsman's Mark Ltd.).

Dentage: 4 ends to the inch.

Weft: Wilton's 2-ply carpet wool, used 5–6 strands.

Draft: Tabby.

Note: the photograph shows the fringes before and after making an Oriental plait and twist.

Plate 15   Sample Wool Rug Weave

Warp: 10/6 ply white cotton twine (Linen Thread Co. Ltd.).

Dentage: 4 ends to the inch, threaded double.

Weft: 6-ply rug wool in dark grey and white (Dryad Handicrafts Ltd.).

Draft: Tabby.

This rug was produced by a variant of the twist method—without the twist. Both colours were simply wound straight on to the shuttle and manipulated in the open shed. The ground was worked with the white wool predominantly on top so as to cover the grey. For the design the grey was brought to the top, in short lengths to begin with, and increasing in each row until it covered the whole warp from edge to edge, then decreasing again till the shape was complete.

The rug is reversible, with the colours reversed on the back.

The 6-ply rug wool used double has produced a very thick and hard-wearing weave.

Plate 14 Rush Mat

Designed and woven by Marlene Frühoff.

Natural rushes, fawn hemp and white cotton were used, the rush plaits being soaked in water at least two hours before use, preferably overnight. This makes them sufficiently pliable to work.

Size: 4 ft. 8 in. × 3 ft. 2½ in.

Warp: White cotton twine.

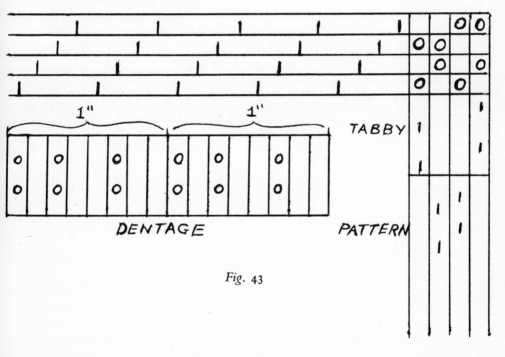

Fig. 43

Dentage: A reed 8 ends to the inch was used with 3 double threads per inch throughout the width. The spacing, starting from the left, is shown in Fig. 43.

Weft: Natural rushes (Jacobs, Young and Westbury Ltd.) pale fawn hemp (from builders' merchants) and white cotton twine, used double.

Draft: see Fig. 43.

Pedals 1 and 4 give the cotton twine tabby, and 2 and 3 the wider spacing for the rushes and part of the hemp. Several tabby rows of white twine were placed on either side of the hemp and rushes to bind them. Very careful attention must be given to the edges as the photograph shows.

Plate 22 Sample Rag Rug Weave in Twill

Warp: 10/6 ply white cotton twine (Linen Thread Co. Ltd.).

Dentage: 4 ends to the inch, threaded double.

Weft: Mixed rags, dark green and dark peacock blue for the narrow dark stripes; pale moss green for the narrow stripes at the beginning and end and the wide stripes in the body of the weave; shocking pink and pale turquoise blue twisted together for the medium stripes in a shot effect.

Draft: Twill, Fig. 44.

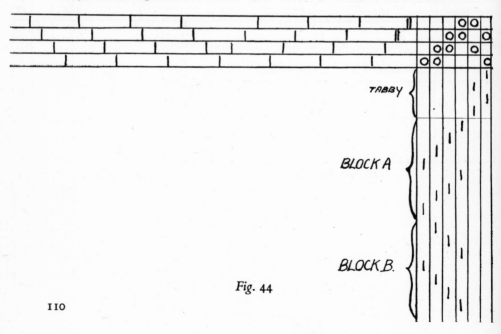

TABBY

BLOCK A

BLOCK B.

Fig. 44

The tabby was used only for the end rows in warp twine. For the twill pattern pedal Block A twice, then Block B twice, and repeat until the rug is complete. To vary the texture one could make some of the stripes, say the narrow dark ones, in tabby.

Plate 23 Sample Weave in Goose-eye

This is a sample weave in tabby and goose-eye. The foundation weave is in blue, with the design in black on a stone ground.

Size: 3 ft. 4 in. × 1 ft. 8 in.

Warp: 10/6 ply cotton twine (Linen Thread Co. Ltd.), dyed black.

Dentage: 4 ends to the inch, threaded double.

Weft: 6-ply Rug Wool, (Dryad Handicrafts, Ltd.)

Draft: See Fig. 45.

Black stripes in tabby. Each end a 2 inch band in blue goose-eye, pedalled 3, 3, 5, 6, 3, 4, 5, 6, repeat twice, then 5, 4, 3, 6, 5, 4, 3, repeat twice. The bottom single row of pattern pedalled 3, 4, 5, 6, 5, 4, 3 with a row of tabby between each pattern throw. The main centre part of the rug is pedalled in big diaper pattern and small alternatively. The pedalling for the big pattern: 3, 4, 5, 6, repeated five times. For the small: 3, 4, 5, 6, 5, 4, 3 only.

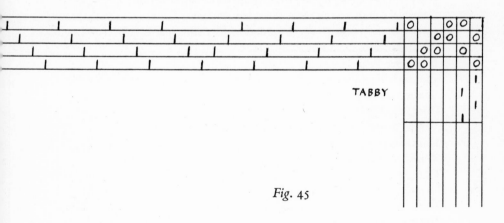

Fig. 45

The top first row of pattern is pedalled: 3, 4, 5, 6, 3, 4, 5, 6, with a tabby throw in the stone colour between each pattern throw. The second row: 6, 5, 4, 3, 6, 5, 4, 3, likewise with a tabby throw in between.

Plate 24 Sample Weave in Rosepath and Tabby

This sample weave is introduced to show some of the effects which can be achieved with a rosepath thread-up simply by varying the pedalling sequences. The draft gives the basic sequence.

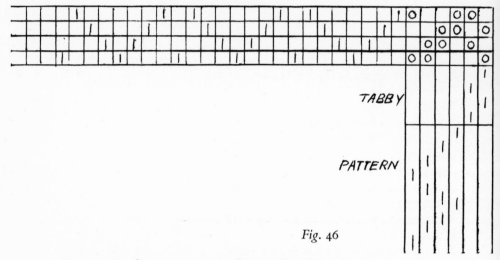

Fig. 46

Warp: 10/6 white cotton twine (Linen Thread Co. Ltd.).

Dentage: 4 ends to the inch, threaded double.

Weft: Mixed cotton rags; foundation in white, pattern in crimson, dark blue, pale blue and emerald green.

Draft: See Fig. 46.

The pedalling sequence, starting from the bottom, was as follows:

White, tabby 4 rows.

Dark, rosepath: 3, 4, 5, 6,

White, rosepath: 3, 4, 5, 6 and repeat for 2 inches.

Dark, rosepath: 6, 3, 4, 5.

White, tabby: 5 rows.

Dark, rosepath: 3, 4, 5, 6, 5, 4, 3.

White, tabby: 4 rows.

Dark and White, alternating, rosepath (6, 4, 6, 4, 6, 4, 6) and tabby.

White, tabby: 3 rows.

Dark and White, alternating, rosepath and tabby: 3, 1, 4, 2, 5, 1, 6, 2; repeat once.

White, tabby; 4 rows.

112

Dark, rosepath: 3, 4, 5, 6.

White, tabby: 4 rows.

Dark and White, alternating, rosepath and tabby: 3, 1, 4, 2, 5, 1, 6, 2, 5, 1, 4, 2, 3, 1.

White, tabby: 5 rows.

Dark, rosepath: 6, 3, 4, 5, 6.

White, tabby: 5 rows.

Plate 29   Wool Rug in Rosepath and Tabby

Designed and woven by Helen Hutton.

A wool rug in shades of black, white, grey, pale yellow and moss green.

Size: 4 ft. × 2 ft. 6 in.

Warp: Linen rug warp (Craftsman's Mark Ltd.).

Dentage: 4 ends to the inch.

Weft: Wilton 6-ply rug wool. Quantity required about 3 lb.

Draft: See Fig. 47.

This rug was made on a home-built 4-shaft, 6-pedal horizontal underslung loom.

After edging with warp string, half an inch of tabby was woven in black. The pattern was commenced by pedalling Block A for a depth of $1\frac{1}{2}$ inches, using two shuttles introduced from opposite sides, one black with No. 4 pedal, the other green on No. 6 pedal. Great care must be taken with the selvedges for this pattern, and the alternating throws twisted round the outer warp thread to give a uniform edge.

Still using Block A, the green on No. 6 pedal was changed to grey for another $1\frac{1}{2}$ inches of depth, and then to yellow for $1\frac{1}{2}$ inches. No. 4 pedal was left in black.

Finally the black was transferred to No. 6 shed and the grey to No. 4 for $1\frac{1}{2}$ inches.

Then followed the Block B pedalling sequence, with white in No. 3 shed and black in No. 5, continued for 1 inch. It is this sequence which gives the white dots, or rather short white lines between the main vertical lines of the rug; it will be seen that it was used again for the 8th, 10th, 12th and finally the 17th horizontal stripe.

Block B completes half the basic pattern, and the other half was then

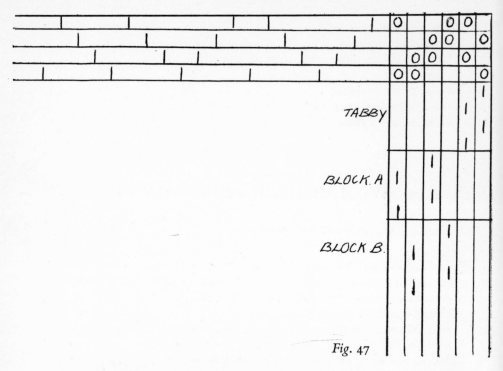

TABBY

BLOCK. A

BLOCK B.

Fig. 47

worked by following the instructions already given, but in the reverse order.

The total sequence can be repeated as often as desired, and of course varied to give different widths of stripes or indeed a different arrangement of Block A and Block B stripes.

The rug is reversible, the back showing an interesting counterchange of this pattern.

Plates 26 and 28
Wool Rug in Honeycomb Weave

Designed and woven by Klares Lewes.

The design of this rug, which is in mushroom pink and black, was suggested by a dry stone wall. Such walls are common enough. This one, as it happens, was seen at the back of a beach in Cornwall, and the design originated as an idle thought while lazing on the sand.

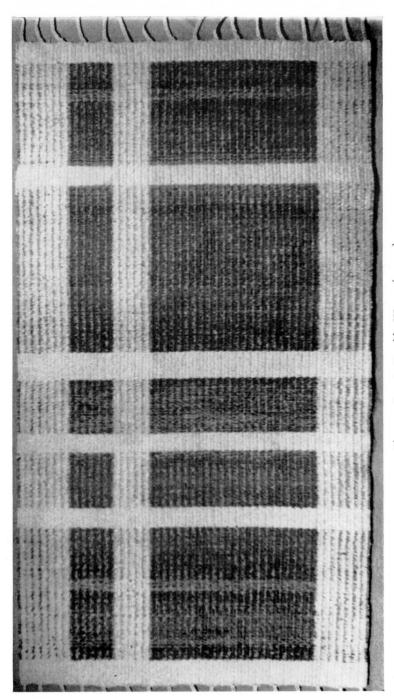

Plate 47 Rug in Double Weave (p. 135)
Designed and woven by Marlene Frühoff

Plate 48 Pebble and Brick Pavement

Plate 49 Chequered Rug in Rosepath and Tabby (p. 136) based on the above photograph
Designed and woven by Helen Hutton

Warp: 10/6 ply cotton twine (Linen Thread Co. Ltd.), dyed black.
Dentage: 4 ends to the inch, threaded double.
Weft: 2-ply carpet wool in black and two tones of mushroom pink.
Draft: See Fig. 48.

The first fourteen threads are on the fourth and third shafts, the next fourteen threads on the second and first shafts. Repeat the sequence as often

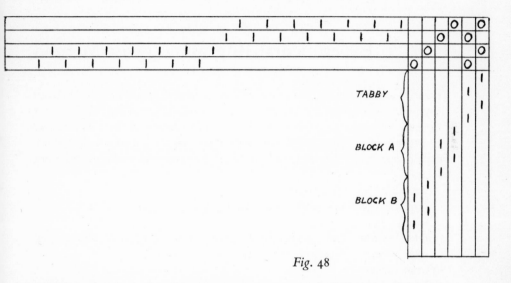

Fig. 48

as necessary for the required width. Pedals 1 and 2 take care of the tabby throws; with a 4-pedal loom the same result is obtained by pressing pedals 1 and 3 simultaneously, then 2 and 4.

Begin and finish with $\frac{1}{2}$ inch in tabby, using the black warp twine.

The pattern is obtained by pedalling the Block A sequence 14 times in mushroom pink, followed by two throws of tabby in black, then Block B 14 times in mushroom pink, followed by two throws of tabby in black. This can be repeated as often as necessary to complete the rug, but if it is desired to introduce some irregularity, as in the rug shown, vary the number of times the sequences are pedalled. In the example this was done by occasionally reducing the number of times the pattern sequences were pedalled, which caused the black in the tabby rows to appear in thick squares. Furthermore, in some places the light-coloured wool was used for the tabby rows, this resulting in a complete break right across the rug.

On the reverse, the weave produces a very 'overshot' appearance rather

117

like that of imitation *Flossa*. The overshot threads, being very firmly held in place, can be cut down the middle and this will give a 'tufted' side which can be used uppermost. If however the rug is intended to be used with the honeycomb side up, then the reverse should be lined.

Plate 33 Experimental Rug using Twist Method

This trial weave is an experiment in the twist method (see Fig. 28). It shows clearly three of the effects that can be obtained by manipulating two different coloured weft threads twisted together, according to whether they are laid in a warp side by side, or one covering the other, or the two left twisted. Further experiment, for instance in the degree of twisting, will give still other effects.

Size: 2 ft. 8 in. × 1 ft. 10 in.

Warp: Grey worsted wool used double (Multiple Fabric Co. Ltd.).

Dentage: 5 ends to the inch.

Weft: Wilton 2-ply carpet wool used in four strands in white, deep green and various shades of crimson.

Draft: Tabby.

The two end sections were woven in crimson and white with four strands of varying crimson and four of white twisted together. Leaving the yarn twisted as it came from the shuttle produced the jaspe ground. The pattern was achieved by untwisting short sections in the warp in a zigzag design and placing the red uppermost to cover the white.

Two bands of tabby separate the end sections from the centre section which is in green and white. It was worked by bringing the twisted yarns to the centre design where they were untwisted and laid side by side over the area. The white was always used uppermost and the green below.

The rug is completely reversible except for the end zigzags which are colour reversed on the back.

For this type of weave it is essential that the threads which are twisted together should be of the same ply or they will not twist properly. Moreover if they are intended to be thick, then it is best to build them up of 2-ply; three or four strands of this will handle more easily than one of 6-ply, particularly when overlaying.

118

Plate 31 Khelim Type Rug

Designed and woven by Helen Hutton.

The rectangular shapes used for this rug were suggested by a newspaper photograph of a group of dining-room furniture (Plate 30). Slight rearrangements were made to balance the design but the basic forms were unchanged. The working out of the pattern shapes was done by the method of colouring rectangles of paper and placing them in various combinations until a pleasing design seemed to result.

The colours, on a ground of pale sage green, were chocolate brown, pale mimosa yellow, deep sky blue and a forest green. Lines of pale grey and white were introduced at irregular intervals to make a variation in the colour of the ground.

Size: 3 ft. 10 in. × 2 ft. 3 in.

Warp: Linen Rug Warp (Craftsman's Mark Ltd.).

Dentage: 4 ends to the inch.

Weft: Wilton 6-ply rug wool was used in the following quantities:

    2 lb. sage green,

    ½ lb. brown,

    ½ lb. forest green,

    ½ lb. yellow,

    ½ lb. blue,

    2 oz. grey,

    2 oz. white.

Draft: Tabby.

The Khelim interlock method is described in Chapter 4. The arrangement of the blocks of colour is shown in Fig. 49 which gives the scale of the rug, four squares representing one inch.

A shuttle is required for each colour, but a small 'dolly' may be used for small areas of inlay.

When joining the weft yarn, cut the ends into long tapers and twist together to avoid undue thickness where the joined ends overlap.

Although this rug was woven on a horizontal loom, fitted with an ordinary batten, a rug comb was also used for closer beating.

A final point to be stressed in the weaving of a rug of this kind is the extreme importance of having the warp very tightly strained and uniformly taut. In addition, the use of a template is almost a necessity. The reason is that the pattern is based on clear-cut rectangles and any irregularities in the weave will cause distortion of the pattern edges.

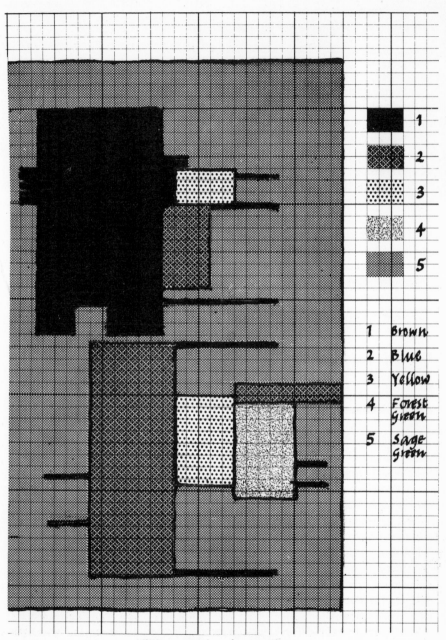

Fig. 49. Colour key to Plate 31

Plate 25 Sample Rag Rug Weave with Spot Pattern Variant

Warp: 10/6 ply white cotton twine (Linen Thread Co. Ltd.).
Dentage: 4 ends to the inch, threaded double.
Weft: foundation—white cotton sheeting pattern—yellow cotton strips, with a small amount of white candlewicking for the narrow broken yellow stripes.
Draft: Tabby.
The method of producing a spot pattern is fully described on page 79. In the present case, by applying it continuously instead of in scattered places, it has been used to produce lengthways stripes instead of spots.

The shed stick was inserted under three warp threads for each stripe.

To produce the breaks in the yellow stripes, candlewicking used double was substituted for the yellow cotton material, four rows for the two outer stripes and three for the narrower inner ones.

Plate 32 Rag Rug in Tabby and Rosepath

Designed and woven by Klares Lewes.

This rug is in black and white stripes, using mainly plain-surfaced materials, but also a proportion of black velvet to produce an interesting change of texture as well as a more intense black.

Size: 3 ft. 9 in. × 2 ft.
Warp: 10/6 ply white cotton twine (Linen Thread Co. Ltd.).
Dentage: 4 ends to the inch.
Weft: Approximately $2\frac{1}{2}$ lb. mixed rags, 1 lb. white, $1\frac{1}{2}$ lb. black and a small quantity of black and white checked material for the white line in the black stripes.

The white material is ordinary sheeting torn in strips about 1 inch wide. The black is a mixture of dull-surfaced woollens and black-out curtain material, as well as the black velvet. For the narrow black stripes only black velvet was used.

Draft: see Fig. 50.

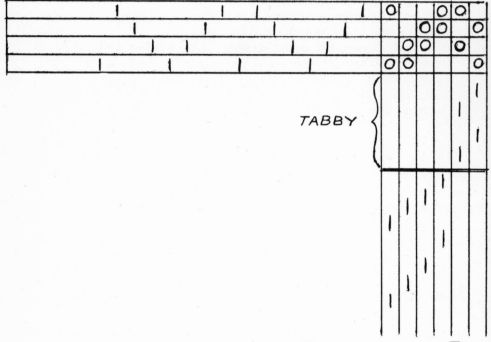

Fig. 50

Begin and finish with 6–8 rows of warp string. The working is as follows:

End stripes in black, 6 inches wide, with the first and last two rows woven in tabby and the remainder in rosepath. The white pattern in the centre is produced by three rows on the No. 6 pedal, using the black and white checked material and alternating with a tabby throw in black.

The wide centre stripes in black are worked in the same way, but are 6½ inches wide.

The two white stripes at each end measure 2½ inches, and those in the centre 1¾ inches. They are woven in tabby.

Lastly the three bands of narrow black and white stripes each measure 2½ inches overall, and are woven in tabby.

Plate 34 Rag Rug with Inlay Pattern

Designed and woven by Klares Lewes.

Mixed rags in shades of midnight blue with an inlay pattern in white.
 Size: 2 ft. 9 in. × 1 ft. 9 in.
 Warp: 10/6 ply cotton twine (Linen Thread Co. Ltd.).

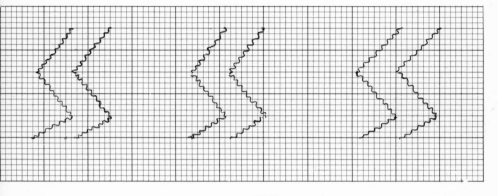

Fig. 51. 1 square = 1 warp thread

Dentage: 4 ends to the inch threaded double.
 Draft: Tabby.
 Inlay: For the working of the inlay see Chapter 5. The arrangement is
 shown in the diagrammatic plan (Fig. 51).

Plate 36 Rag Rug with Inlay Pattern

Designed and woven by Klares Lewes.

Woven in mixed rags in shades of dark blue and emerald green. The inlay
pattern is in white and pale blue.
 Size: 3 ft. 9 in. × 1 ft. 10 in.
 Warp: 10/6 ply cotton twine (Linen Thread Co. Ltd.).
 Dentage: 4 ends to the inch, threaded double.
 Weft: Cotton and woollen rags, approximately 2 lb.
 Draft: Tabby.

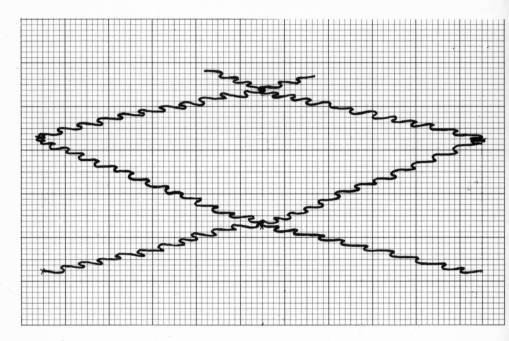

Fig. 52. 1 square=1 warp thread

Fig. 52 shows the arrangement of the inlay, the vertical lines of squares representing doubled warp threads.

Weave 2½ inches in tabby with mixed rags of blue and emerald which are the ones used throughout for the ground. Now start the inlay with the right-hand band in white, and the left-hand one in pale blue. Place the pattern weft in the open shed after the ground blue has been laid in, secure the strip under a warp thread, then pass it over two warp threads of the raised shed and finish under the next thread. In the next and each succeeding row move the pattern strip three or four warp threads over towards the opposite side. Where the strips cross they will overlap partially for a few rows till they have moved away from each other.

When the opposite limits have been reached, continue the pattern vertically in a straight line for about 2 inches, then proceed as before but shifting the pattern strips gradually in the other direction.

Plate 35   Rag Rug with Inlay Pattern

Designed and woven by Klares Lewes.

This rug, woven in mixed rags, presents a very simple inlay in white on a peacock blue ground.

Size: 3 ft. 6 in. × 1 ft. 9 in.

Warp: 10/6 ply white cotton twine (Linen Thread Co. Ltd.).

Dentage: 4 ends to the inch, threaded double.

Weft: Mixed rags.

Draft: Rosepath and tabby (see Fig. 53).

The body of the rug is in tabby, but 2 inches at the beginning and end have been worked in rosepath pedalled 6, 4, 6, 4.

TABBY

PATTERN

Fig. 53

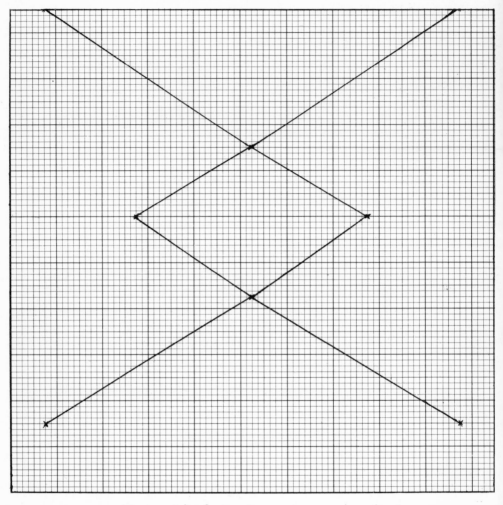

Fig. 53a. Inlay for Rag Rug..1 square=1 warp thread

The arrangement of the inlay is shown for half the rug in Fig. 53a, in which each line of small squares from top to bottom represents one warp thread, and the sides of the large squares represent 2 inches. The working method will be found fully described in the instructions for the rug on Plate 34 (page 83).

Plate 37   Tapestry and Tufted Rug

Designed and woven by Ronald Grierson, F.S.I.A.

This very successful rug, worked in shades of black, yellow ochre and white, on a 2 shaft foot pedal upright loom, shows very clearly what striking effects can be achieved by the simplest means.

Size: 5 ft. 6 in. × 3 ft.
Warp: White cotton, approximately 1 lb.
Dentage: 4 ends to the inch, used double.
Weft: Dyed black wool with every 8th row in undyed black wool, approximately 7 lb.
Tufts of yellow ochre and white, approximately 1½ lb.
Draft: Tabby.

Plate 38   Tapestry and Tufted Rug

Designed and woven by Ronald Grierson, F.S.I.A.

This rug shows rectangular shapes in grey and black placed irregularly on a white ground.

Size: 5 ft. × 3 ft.
Warp: White cotton, used double, 1 lb.
Dentage: 4 ends to the inch.
Weft: Ground in white wool, approximately 6 lb. Tufts in a mixture of natural grey and natural black wool. Approximately 2 lb. each.
Draft: Tabby.

Plate 39   Rya Rug

Designed and woven by Anne Meurling.

Handtufted *Rya* Rug in white, off-white and black.
Size: 9 ft. × 6 ft. 8 in.
Warp: Barbour's Champion Seaming Grey 3c.
Dentage: 6 ends per inch. Weight of warp: approx. 3 lb.
Weft: 2-ply carpet wool (Craftsman's Mark Ltd.) with a small amount of linen and cotton in the tufting.
Weight of rug: Approximately 23½ lb.

This rug is tufted by the long pile method (see Chapter 6), with tufts approximately 3 inches long. The warp is fully covered by the weft. There are about 18 rows of tabby to each row of tufting, making 1 inch of weave.

Plate 40 Tufted Rug

Designed by Marianne Straub, F.S.I.A.

A tufted rug in white and natural brown. The design consists of 3 inch-wide stripes made up with the brown and white alternately predominant by using a mixture in the tufts of 7 brown to 1 white or 7 white to 1 brown strand.
Size: 5 ft. 6 in. ×2 ft. 9 in.
Warp: White Welsh 2-ply wool.
Dentage: 11 ends to the inch, used double.
Weft: 2-ply Welsh wool, white and natural brown.
Draft: Twill (see p. 66, Fig. 20).
1 row of tufting to 8 rows of twill, i.e. 8 picks between tufts.
This rug, so simple, in appearance, owes its effectiveness to the sensitive handling of the transitions from light to dark. From a technical point of view it will be noticed that the foundation weave is in twill instead of tabby.
Of particular interest is the fact that it was woven in 1936, in use since 1940, and shows no signs of wear.

Plate 41 Tufted Rug

Designed and woven by Mary Patten, Cert. Des. R.C.A.

Tufted rug of squares and rectangles in tones of orange, green and brown on a white ground.
Size: 5 ft. 6 in. ×4 ft.
Warp: Cotton.
Dentage: 4 ends per inch.
Weft: 6-ply wool (white) for ground.
Tufts: Approximately 6 inches long, 6 strands to each tuft.
Draft: Tabby.
Weight of rug: 12 lb.

Plate 50 Tapestry Rug (p. 137)
Designed and woven by Anne Meurling

Plate 51 *Rya Rug* (*p.* 138)

Designed by John Hutton and woven by Helen Hutton

Loom: Upright 2-pedal Rug Loom, 3 ft. 4 in. (Kensington Weavers Ltd.)

The tufts are unusually long—about 6 inches, and are made up of six strands. There are six rows of tabby to each row of tufts.

Plate 43   *Rya* Rug

Designed and woven by Brian Knight, Des. R.C.A., F.R.S.A.

This rug shows squares in tones of geranium red, orange and purple on a tufted background in blue, green and purple.

Size: 4 ft. 8 in. × 2 ft. 10 in.

Warp: White warping cotton (Dryad Handicrafts Ltd.), dyed black.

Dentage: 4 ends to the inch.

Weft: For the tabby foundation Paton's black Turkey rug wool was used. The tufts, 1–1½ inches long (using cut lengths of 3 in.–3½ in.), with 3 strands in each tuft, are in Wilton 2-ply carpet wool, white dyed to shade.

Draft: Tabby.

This rug was worked on a Dryad Rug-Weaving Frame, 7 ft. × 4 ft. Each row of tufting is followed by 6–8 rows of tabby, and it will be seen in the photograph how well these are hidden beneath the tufts, though their black will still contribute to the general tone of the rug.

Plate 42   Sample Weave in Imitation *Flossa*

Imitation *Flossa* produces a surface which on a casual inspection is indistinguishable from that of a hand-tufted rug. Characteristic, however, in its appearance is the series of parallel lines along the length of the weave. Similar lines can be produced in hand-tufting, but they cannot be avoided in imitation *Flossa*, and are clearly shown in the completed portion of the rug on Plate 42. The process is very much quicker to work than tufting, but since the tufts are not knotted, the result is probably not as hard-wearing.

Warp: 10/6 white cotton twine (Linen Thread Co. Ltd.).

Dentage: 12 ends to the inch, threaded double.

Weft: Foundation in 10/6 white cotton twine used double. Pattern in candlewicking, pink for the body and white for the narrow stripe.

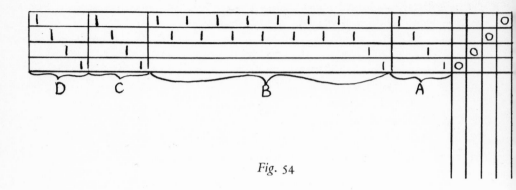

Fig. 54

Draft: See Fig. 54.

Block A for the right selvedge, thread once.

Block B for the body, repeat the number of times required for the width

Block C, thread once on the last repeat to balance the pattern.

Block D, thread once for the left selvedge.

Pedalling: Tabby—Pedal 1, 3 simultaneously.

2, 4 simultaneously.

On a 6-pedal loom the shafts can, of course, be tied additionally to the two extra pedals to produce the tabby weave.

Pattern, woven with a tabby binder:

1, 3 simultaneously (cotton twine)

3, 4 simultaneously (candlewicking)

2, 4 simultaneously (cotton twine)

3, 4 simultaneously (candlewicking)

Repeat the sequence as often as necessary.

Use two shuttles, one for the cotton twine and one for the candlewicking. Begin and end the rug with 2 inches of cotton twine in tabby.

Lay the candlewicking very loosely in the shed and pull back between the upper threads of the shed so as to form a series of loops running like waves across the rug. These loops, which are clearly shown in the right-hand half of the photograph, should be as nearly alike as possible.

Each throw of candlewicking is followed by one of tabby.

When the rug is off the loom, insert a thin stick with a pointed end lengthways into each row of loops, and slash down the centre with a razor-blade.

The left-hand half of the photograph shows the finished result.

132

Plate 44 Tufted Rug

Designed and woven by Klares Lewes.

A long-pile tufted rug in three shades of orange, three of deep red, and two of purple.

Size: 3 ft. 2 in. × 2 ft.

Warp: Rug Linen Warp (Craftsman's Mark Ltd.).

Dentage: 4 ends to the inch.

Weft: Wilton's 2-ply carpet wool. Approximately 2 lb. of wool, about ¼ lb. of each shade is required.

Draft: Tabby.

The rug is begun and finished with 6 rows of warp string. For the tabby background use 3 strands of wool in mixed dark shades. The tufts, 2½ inches long, are also made up of 3 strands of mixed colours, and are knotted in the open shed.

Fig. 55 is a diagrammatic plan of the rug in which each line of squares from top to bottom corresponds to one warp thread. Measured vertically each square equals ½ inch. It will be seen that the edges of the rug are left untufted, and here alongside the blocks of tufting it will be necessary to run extra tabby threads to compensate for the bulk of the tufting. It will probably be necessary also to pad out the borders on the cloth roller with folds of newspaper in order to maintain even warp tension (see Chapter 6).

The body of the rug begins and ends with 1 inch in tabby.

The first tufted shape measures 3 inches in height at the base. Begin with a few tufts at the base end, gradually increasing the number in each row until at ¾ inch the left-hand point has been reached. Repeat for ½ inch, then decrease gradually until the shape is complete.

Both this cone and the last cone are very narrow. For this reason every row is tufted (remember, however, that tufting is *always* based on tabby, which means that each row of tufting is preceded by a tabby throw and in the open shed method is knotted in the same shed). In the remaining cones 3 rows of tabby are worked after every fourth row of tufting.

The base cone is followed by an inch of tabby.

The first row of cones measures 12 inches in height. Use 5 tufts for the broad bases, 2 tufts for the points. The broad bases are gradually decreased to 2 tufts, and the points gradually increased to 5 tufts.

The remaining cones have the same base and point measurements, but their height is 8 inches in the second row and 6 inches in the last row.

Work one inch in tabby between each block.

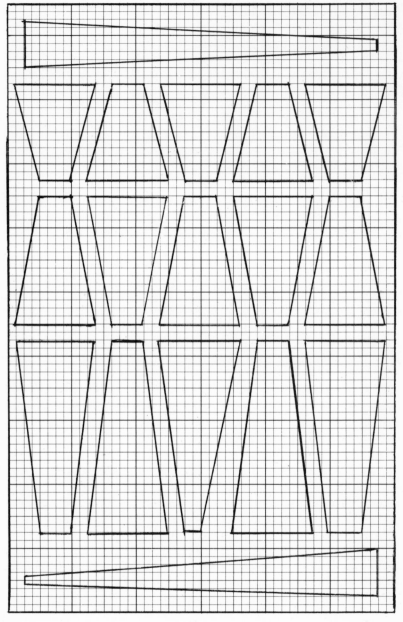

Fig. 55

Plate 47 Rug in Double Weave

Designed and woven by Marlene Frühoff.

Double weave with design reversed on the back. On a pale grey-blue foundation, a block pattern in royal blue, sky blue, turquoise and violet. Some of the blocks are in a single shade, others are toned by mixing.

Size: 5 ft. 2 in. × 2 ft. 10 in.
Warp: Linen Rug Warp (Craftsman's Mark Ltd.).
Dentage: 4 ends to the inch.
Weft: Wilton's Rug Wool used double.
Draft: The draft is shown in Fig. 56. The vertical stripes are produced by the threading of the warp and the combination used for the rug illustrated was as follows (from right to left):
Block A, repeated 7 times, followed by
Block B, 21 times;
Block A, 5 times;
Block B, 6 times;
Block A, 7 times.

The thread-up must always finish with the two end threads shown; it will be seen that they are, in fact, the same as the first two threads in each of the two blocks, so that they can be added to whatever happens to be used last without affecting the pattern.

The three outer threads on either side are doubled for the selvedge.

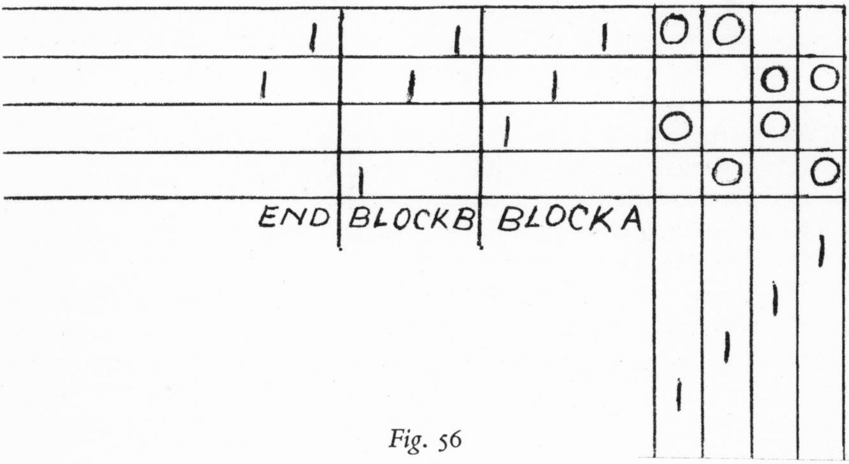

Fig. 56

Two shuttles carrying different colours are used for alternate throws, always coming in from opposite sides.

Begin by weaving two inches in grey foundation, double stranded, then start the colour blocks by throwing alternate rows in turquoise and violet (single strands twisted together produce the broken colour effect) and in grey. Work for thirteen inches, keeping to the foundation grey but varying the twisting of the coloured strands slightly so as to give patches of colour rather than a jaspe effect.

Then follow $2\frac{1}{2}$ inches in foundation grey, 6 inches in blues, 2 inches in grey, $5\frac{1}{2}$ inches in blues, 3 inches in grey and the last colour block $10\frac{1}{2}$ inches in blues. Finish off with 2 inches in grey.

The back shows the pattern in reverse.

Double weave is capable of an infinite number of variations simply by altering the combination of blocks A and B in width or in location. The blending threads were used for the sake of the interesting colour areas which could be produced, but simple colours can, of course, be used perfectly well for the colour blocks.

Plates 48 and 49
Chequered Rug in Rosepath and Tabby

Designed and woven by Helen Hutton.

This rug, in a pattern of 10 inch squares in black and white, was suggested by the wall illustrated on Plate 48.

Though the strip shown is complete in itself, the motif is intended to be a unit design, suitable for a large rug in an all-over pattern made up of a number of strips joined together.

Size: 5 ft. × 2 ft. 6in.

Warp: White cotton twine (Linen Thread Co. Ltd.).

Dentage: 4 ends to the inch, threaded double.

Weft: 6-ply rug wool (Wilton) in black and white.

Draft: See Fig. 57.

The weave is in black tabby squares alternating with white squares in rosepath, but the centre portion of the black squares is relieved by a rosepath patterning. The squares are interlocked by the Khelim method (see Chapter 4).

First row: For the black tabby squares use the pedalling sequence shown in Block 1 of the draft.

136

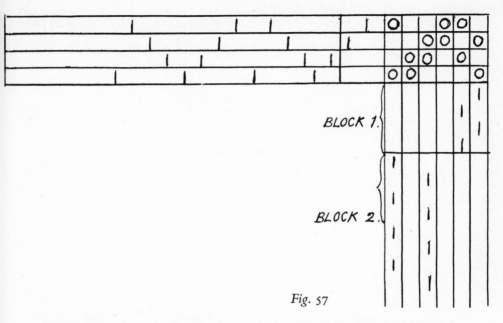

BLOCK 1.

BLOCK 2.

Fig. 57

The white square is pedalled in accordance with Block 2, using white wool for No. 6 pedal and black wool for No. 4.

Second Row. The white square as in the first row. For the black square pedal Block 1 for 1½ inches, then four rows of Block 2 with black for No. 6 pedal and white for No. 4. Repeat the sequence four times, ending with 1½ inches in black, Block 1.

Remaining Rows. Repeat first and second rows.

Plate 50 Tapestry Rug

Designed and woven by Anne Meurling.

Plain tapestry weave in purple, reddish brown, pink, green-blue with patterning in black.

Size: 5 ft. × 3 ft. 4 in.
Warp: Cotton fishing net twine.
Dentage: 6 ends per inch.
Weft: Hair yarn (cowhair and wool mixed) from the Swedish Hemslöjd, not home dyed.

Draft: Tabby.

Weight of rug: 5½ lb.

Loom: Woven on a loom made by the weaver's great-grandfather for her grandmother about 1880.

Plate 51   Rya Rug

Designed by John Hutton, woven by Helen Hutton.

Hand tufting in black, grey, lime, apricot, orange-pink and grey-mauve on a grey ground.

Size: 31 in. × 52 in.

Warp: Linen rug warp (Craftsman's Mark Ltd.) approx. ¾ lb.

Dentage: 4 ends to the inch.

Weft: Wilton's 2-ply carpet wool, approx. 4 lb.

Draft: Tabby.

The complexity of the design necessitated special steps. It was first traced in outline and, with the tracing supported under the warp, the lines were marked in ink on to the warp threads. Some six inches or so were done at a time, and about an inch left untufted to which the following section of tracing could be keyed. The original cartoon was suspended immediately in front of the upper cross-bar of the loom, an under-slung horizontal loom, and used as a guide to colour.

The tufts are four-stranded, 2 inches in length, and secured, using the Turkish knot. Six rows of grey tabby foundation follow every four rows of tufting.

Plate 52   Khelim Rug

Designed and woven by Mrs. E. G. Mullins.

Tapestry Rug. A Khelim pattern in black with white edging on a red ground, the ends edged in grey.

Size: Approx. 2 ft. 6 in. × 4 ft. 6 in.

Warp: Heavy linen.

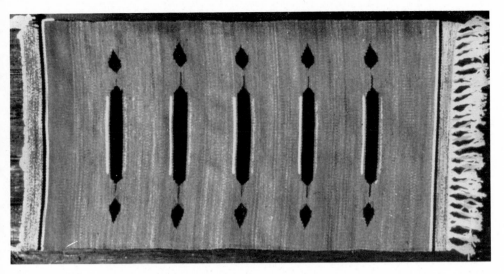

Plate 52 Khelim Rug (*p. 138*)
Designed and woven by Mrs. E. G. Mullins

Plate 53 Khelim Rug (*p. 141*)
Designed and woven by Barbara Mullins

Plate 54 Warp and Weft Rug, 'Black and White' (p. 141)
Designed and woven by Tadek Beutlich

Dentage: 5 ends per inch.
Weft: 2-ply carpet wool (Craftsman's Mark Ltd.).
Draft: Tabby

Plate 53 Khelim Rug

Designed and woven by Barbara Mullins.

Tapestry Rug. A Khelim pattern in black and brown on off-white ground, the ends striped black and brown.
   Size: Approx. 4 ft. 6 in. × 2 ft. 6 in.
   Warp: Heavy Linen.
   Dentage: 5 ends per inch.
   Weft: 2-ply carpet wool (Craftsman's Mark Ltd.).
   Draft: Tabby.

Plate 54

Warp and Weft Rug, 'Black and White'

Designed and woven by Tadek Beutlich.

The warp face technique has already been illustrated on Plate 10 where it is used to produce a predominantly lengthways stripe. In this interesting rug, warp face has been combined with the ordinary technique to produce not a continuous stripe but a series of irregular rectangular pattern shapes. Such a rug is known as a 'warp rib and weft rib' or 'warp and weft' for short, 'weft rib' being the alternative name for 'warp face' because of the cross ribbing it produces and 'warp rib' the alternative name for the ordinary weaves, such as tabby, which produce a lengthways ribbing. An advantage of warp face technique is that it produces an extremely thick and hard-wearing rug.
   Warp: 2-ply carpet wool.
   Dentage: 22 ends to the inch.
   Weft: Jute, dyed black, and 2-ply carpet wool.

Draft: Thread-up: 4, 3, 4, 3, 4, 3; 2, 1, 2, 1, 2, 1, repeat.
    Tie-up (using four pedals):
        Shafts 1 and 3 to pedal 1
        Shafts 2 and 4 to pedal 2
        Shafts 1 and 2 to pedal 3
        Shafts 3 and 4 to pedal 4
For warp rib: pedal 2, 1.
For weft rib: pedal 4, 3.

A Home-made Loom

FIG. 58 SHOWS the loom, a horizontal under-slung type with four shafts and six pedals, on which all but the most complicated kind of work, necessitating six or more shafts, can be produced. And if the weaver should ever wish to extend his activity into this field, there will be no great difficulty in adding extra shafts and pedals.

Construction is sectional, enabling the loom to be taken apart for ease of storage. No difficult joints are involved, but it is important that they should be reasonably well-fitting, for the batten or beater imposes a considerable strain on the frame so that looseness in the joints will soon show itself in a distressing rocking and in difficulties with the warp.

The recommended timber is pine, straight-grained and free from knots, and modest in price. It is very easy to work and looks business-like and attractive when finished off in varnish.

The overall dimensions given, which are finished sizes, are for a 4 ft. loom, but they can be varied within reasonable limits to suit individual ambition and available space.

THE SIDE FRAMES (FIG. 59)

The side frames form individual units, both identical though reversed in relation to each other, save that the left frame—which is the one illustrated —makes simple provision for a detachable iron rod to carry the four lams, while the right-hand one has screwed to it the ratchets controlling the two rollers.

For the sake of clarity these ratchets, numbered 6, are in fact shown in the illustration. Their precise location on the inside of the right-hand frame will depend on the ratchet wheels actually used for the rollers.

A batten stop, consisting of a short length of $\frac{3}{8}$ inch dowelling, is socketed and glued into the outside of the frame. It is shown in Fig. 58.

The joints of the frames, being permanent, are glued stub tenons.

THE CROSS-PIECES

The frames themselves are held together by the top cross-piece (Fig. 60); at waist level by the breast beam, cloth beam and roller beam (Fig. 61); and at the foot by the two cross-pieces (Fig. 62); the joints used are blind dove-tails for the three beams and stub tenons for the three cross-pieces. The dove-

VIEW OF LOOM

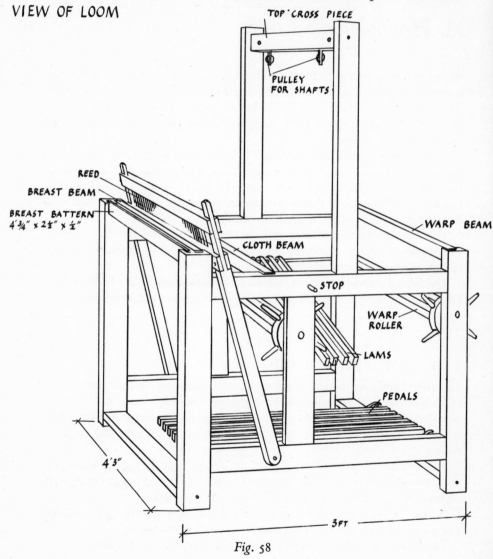

TOP CROSS PIECE

PULLEY FOR SHAFTS

REED

BREAST BEAM

BREAST BATTERN
4'¾" x 2½" x ¼"

CLOTH BEAM

WARP BEAM

STOP

WARP ROLLER

LAMS

PEDALS

4'3"

3FT

Fig. 58

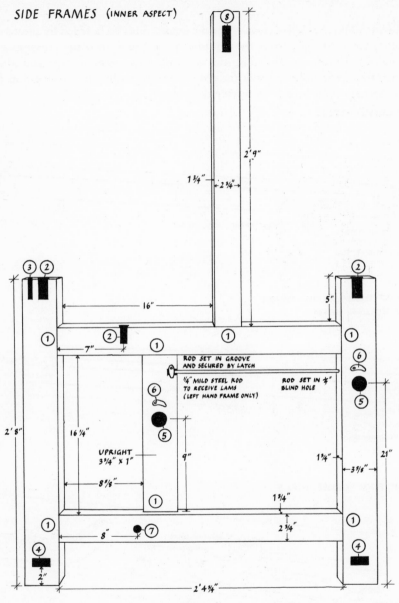

SIDE FRAMES (INNER ASPECT)

Fig. 59

(1) *Glued stub tenon joints.* (2) *Blind dovetails to receive warp beam, cloth beam and breast beam.* (3) *Slot to receive breast batten.* (4) *Holes to receive the stub tenons of foot cross-pieces.* (5) *Holes to receive roller pins.* (6) *Roller ratchets (right-hand only).* (7) $\frac{3}{8}''$ *hole for bolt and wing-nut securing batten.* (8) *Hole to receive stub tenon of top crosspiece*

tails are, of course, self-securing, but the tenons must be fastened by means of bolts passed through from the outside of the frame into the cross-pieces. Suitable holes must be drilled for this with the cross-pieces in place, and additional transverse holes cut into the cross-pieces to enable the locking nuts to be inserted in place ready to receive the bolts.

TOP CROSS-PIECE

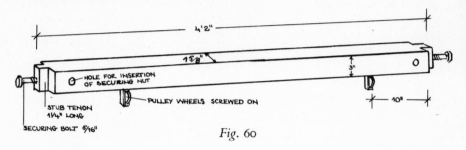

Fig. 60

BREAST BEAM, CLOTH BEAM
AND ROLLER BEAM

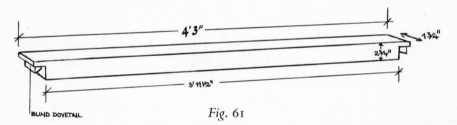

Fig. 61

REAR FOOT CROSS-PIECE

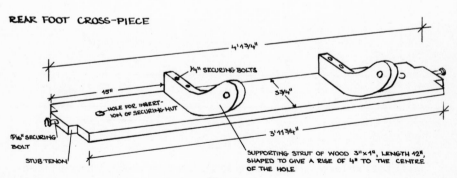

Fig. 62

146

The front foot cross-piece is plain; the rear one (Fig. 62) has bolted to it two pieces of wood forming brackets to support a length of $\frac{1}{2}$ inch mild steel rod on which the pedals are pivoted. The rod is held in place by means of a split pin inserted into a small hole drilled transversely at each end.

The last cross-piece to be mentioned is the breast batten, the ends of which are merely slotted into the frames. It does not help to hold the side frames together and can be omitted; its real purpose being to prevent the finished weave from getting marked when the weaver presses forward against it: in Aubusson in France, where they have been weaving tapestries for centuries, the weavers prefer to place a cushion to rest against.

THE ROLLERS (FIG. 63)

Both the rollers are identical and are made of 4 inch square material, with the corners planed down to produce an octagonal section. Both ends are reduced to pins $1\frac{3}{4}$ inch in diameter for housing in the side frames. The left-hand end seen from the back, has in addition a square section worked on it to receive the ratchet wheel.

ROLLER

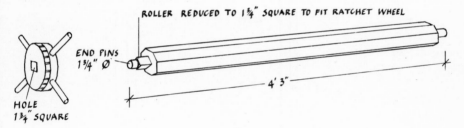

ROLLER REDUCED TO $1\frac{3}{4}$" SQUARE TO FIT RATCHET WHEEL

END PINS
$1\frac{3}{4}$" Ø

HOLE
$1\frac{3}{4}$" SQUARE

4' 3"

Fig. 63

If the particular situation in the workroom renders this more convenient for operation, there is no difficulty in arranging for the ratchet wheels and ratchet to be carried on the other side of the loom.

The ratchet wheel can be made of an oak disc 7 inches in diameter and 2 inches thick obtained from a timber yard. The teeth, $\frac{3}{4}$ inch wide, are worked on one side to a depth of $\frac{1}{4}$ inch. Better still would be to screw a $\frac{1}{4}$ inch steel plate with teeth made by the blacksmith to a somewhat thinner wood disc.

The handles 5 inches long and $\frac{7}{8}$ inch in diameter, are sunk to a depth of 1 inch.

THE BATTEN OR BEATER (Fig. 64)

The cross-bars of the beater are grooved lengthways on the inner edges to receive the reed. The ends are slotted on to the uprights which are reduced to 1 inch for this purpose. The lower bar is glued and screwed to the up-rights. The upper bar is merely a sliding fit but can be secured by means of two wooden pegs.

THE BATTEN OR BEATER

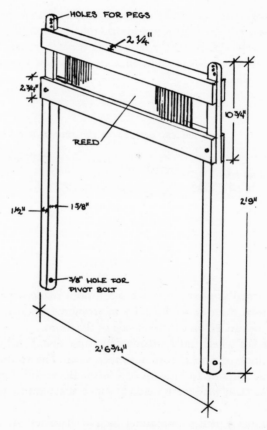

Fig. 64

THE LAMS (FIG. 65)

Four will be needed, cut from $\frac{3}{4}$ in. $\times \frac{7}{8}$ in. beech drilled at one end to pivot on a $\frac{1}{4}$ inch mild steel rod fastened to the left-hand frame as shown in Fig. 59. The lams are separated on the rod by wooden spacing washers, which can be $\frac{1}{2}$ inch dowelling suitably drilled. The spacers should be so arranged that when the lams are in place each is directly beneath one of the shafts.

Each lam should have six holes drilled into it, large enough to enable a doubled piece of cord to be passed through, and so positioned that each hole comes immediately above one of the pedals when the lam is mounted and held horizontally by being tied to one of the shafts.

LAM

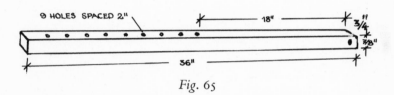

Fig. 65

THE PEDALS (FIG. 66)

Six are required of beech measuring $1\frac{1}{8} \times 1\frac{3}{8}$ in., drilled at one end for pivoting on a $\frac{1}{2}$ inch mild steel rod fastened to the rear cross-bar. The pedals are separated on the rod by means of wooden spacing washers. Like the lams, they have holes drilled through them through which the cord of the lam can be passed and secured.

PEDAL

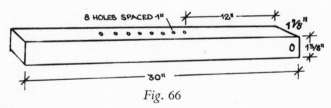

Fig. 66

THE SHAFTS

The shafts are plain lengths of wood measuring approximately $1\frac{1}{4}$ in. $\times \frac{5}{8}$ in. thick and 3 ft. 10 in. long. Eight are needed: they will be paired by means of the heddles and supported from the top cross-bar by the pulleys shown in Fig. 58.

THE FINISH

This calls for no particular comment save that all working surfaces and corners on which string or yarn might catch or fray should be well smoothed with sandpaper and rounded. While the wood can be left raw, it helps to reduce wear on warp and weft, not to mention shaft and pedal ties, if the loom is finally varnished or painted.

Bibliography

BLACK, MARY E. *Key to Weaving.*
  The Bruce Publishing Co., Milwaukee, 1945. A textbook of handweaving techniques and pattern drafts for the beginner. Very detailed and useful. Clear descriptions.
COATES, HELEN. *Weaving for Amateurs.*
  Studio Publications, London.
DAVENPORT, ELSIE. *Your Handweaving.*
  Sylvan Press, London.
  A short useful handbook on elements of weaving.
GALLINGER, OSMA, C. *The Joy of Weaving.*
  Laurel Publishers, Scranton, U.S.A., 1950. A step-by-step book of weaving for the beginner, containing a short section on rugs.
GRIERSON, RONALD, F.S.I.A. *Handwoven Rugs.*
  Dryad Press, Leicester.
  Many techniques applicable to rug-making on the Upright Loom clearly and concisely explained.
HOOPER, LUTHER. *Handloom Weaving.*
  Pitman, London, 1920.
  An early but standard handbook on weaving.
INGERS, GERTRUD. *Nya Matter.*
  I.C.A. Förlaget, Västeras, Sweden, 1959.
  Very clear diagrams and designs.
LEWES, K. AND HUTTON, H. *Your Rugmaking.*
  Sylvan Press, London, 1949.
MAIRET, ETHEL. *Handweaving Today.*
  Faber & Faber, Ltd., London.
  A classic book on the approach to weaving.
MONTELL-GLANTZBERG. *Vävboken.*
  Albert Bonniers Förlag, Stockholm, Sweden, 1925.
SKERI-MATTSON, A. AND OSVALD, I. *I Vävstolen,* I, II.
  Lantbruksförbundets Tidskriftsaktiebolag, Sweden.
WORST, ERNEST F. *Foot Power Loom Weaving.*
  The Bruce Publishing Co., Milwaukee, Wis., U.S.A.
  A very comprehensive publication on all aspects of weaving including loom construction.

List of Suppliers

Linen Thread Co. Ltd., Hilden House, Parry Street, London, S.W.8.
  Warp string in great variety of qualities.
Jacobs, Young & Westbury, Ltd., 199, Borough High St., London, S.E.1.
  Varieties of rushes for matting; loom cord.
Southwick & Case, Ltd., 38, Canning Place, Liverpool 1.
  Suppliers of hemp warp twine, white cotton warp twine, jute yarn 6-and 8-ply,
  loom cords and heddle twine.
J. & W. Stuart, Ltd., Esk Mills, Musselburgh, Scotland.
  Netting twine.
Craftsman's Mark Ltd., Broadlands, Shortheath, Farnham, Surrey.
  Linen rug warp. Welsh wools.
Weaver's Shop Ltd., Wilton Royal Carpet Factory, Wilton, near Salisbury, Wiltshire.
  Rug wool, 2-ply and 6-ply in very large range of colours. Flax warp twine.
Stoddarts (Halifax) Ltd., Empire Works, Halifax, Yorkshire.
  Suppliers of rug wools in 2-ply and 6-ply.
Multiple Fabric Co. Ltd., Dudley Hill, Bradford 4.
  Suppliers of weaving yarns in horsehair, human hair, camel hair, white and grey
  wool yarns. Suitable for warp and weft.
John Keenan & Co. Ltd., 64 Little Horton Lane, Bradford 5.
  Worsted yarn in 2-ply, oiled or scoured.
Dryad Handicrafts Ltd., Leicester.
  Rug wools, looms and all handweaving equipment.
John Maxwell, Folders Lane, Burgess Hill, Sussex.
  Looms and weaving appliances.
The London School of Weaving, 136 Kensington Church St., London, W.8
  All weaving equipment and yarns.
E. J. Arnold & Son, Ltd., Butterley Street, Leeds 10.
  All weaving equipment.

Glossary

Batten or Beater: Part of the loom. A heavy wood frame holding the reed and used to beat the weft so as to compress it (p. 19).

Breast Beam: Front upper cross beam of horizontal loom (p. 144).

Bobbin: Spool carrying yarn (p. 33).

Bobbin Winder: A device used to wind yarn on to spools (p. 33).

Binder: A tabby weft thread introduced into tufted weaves and certain of the looser pattern weaves in order to give strength and firmness to the structure.

'Beaming On': The act of transferring the chained warp to the loom (p. 49).

Castles: Wooden holders used to support the shafts while the warp is being threaded up (p. 32).

'Chaining the Warp': A process of looping the warp while it is being taken from the warping mill or board so as to prevent it getting tangled (p. 48).

Cops: Wound spools of yarn or string as sold from the mills.

Count: The length per lb. of yarns varying with the intrinsic weight of the yarn and its thickness (p. 43).

Cross: The cross-over of threads worked into the warp when it is being laid on the warping mill for the purpose of preventing subsequent tangling, and to ensure that the threads are threaded up on the loom in the order in which they were laid (p. 46). Two crosses are worked, one at the beginning of the warp, known as the Parrey cross, and one at the end, known as the Porrey cross.

Cuts: An expression used when calculating number of yards of linen yarn to the lb. (p. 43).

Cut length method: Process of knotting short lengths of wool yarn into the warp (p. 88).

Dent: Spaces in the reed through which the warp is threaded (p. 28). The character of a reed is defined by reference to the number of dents it has to the inch.

Dentage: The number of dents per inch used for the warp threads; in other words the measure of the spacing of the warp threads on the loom (p. 28).

Dolly: Yarn wound up in neat little skeins (p. 32).

Double Weave: A particular weave technique (p. 76).

'Dressing the Loom': Preparing the loom in readiness for weaving (Chapter 3).

Draft: Diagrammatic analysis of the structure of the weave (p. 63).

Ends: The threads in a warp.

Figure-of-Eight Technique: A method of strengthening the selvedges of a tufted rug (p. 87).

Floats: Loose weft threads stretched over several warp threads, either purposely as in an overshot weave, or as a result of a mistake in the thread-up.

Flossa: Scandinavian word denoting a particularly closely tufted type of rug (p. 93).

Frame Loom: A simple type of loom (p. 21).

Ground Work: Foundation weave surrounding a pattern weave.

Heddles: Short lengths of cotton twine or wire knotted or twisted so as to form three loops and used to support the warp threads in the shafts (p. 23).

Heddle eye: Centre loop of the heddle through which the warp thread is passed.

Heddle Gauge: Jig or frame on which heddles are made (p. 23).

Heddle Horses: Short lengths of wood used as an alternative to pulleys from which the heddle shafts are suspended in such a way so as to enable them to move up and down (p. 56).

Heddle Shafts: Wooden laths on which the heddles are looped (p. 23).

Horizontal Loom: A loom on which the warp is stretched horizontally (p. 19).

Imitation Flossa: A method of producing a tufted effect by weaving a series of floats that are subsequently cut to form the pile (p. 93).

Inlay: Pattern produced by laying in a different weft colour on top of the ground colour (p. 86).

Interlock: A method of creating pattern used in Röllakan and Khelim rugs (p. 74).

Khelim: Rugs of Oriental origin in tapestry weave with inlay (p. 74).

Knotted Rugs: Rugs in which tufts are knotted on a foundation weave to form a raised pile.

Lams: Parts of the loom enabling two or more shafts to be tied to each pedal (p. 24).

'Laying the Warp': The process of preparing the warp and transferring it to the loom (p. 45).

Leashes: Single loops of cotton twine used in place of heddles on the frame loom (p. 21).

Leas: A yardage measure of linen (p. 43).

Overshot Weave: A method of passing the weft over several warp threads in such a way as to form a pattern (p. 93).

Overslung loom: A type of loom on which the batten is suspended from the upper part of the frame (p. 19).

Parrey Cross: see Cross.

'Pedalling': The depressing of the pedals in sequence to form a weave pattern (p. 60).

Pick: A single throw of weft yarn through the shed.

Ply: The number of strands composing wool or cotton yarn.

Porrey Cross: see Cross.

Raddle: A kind of wooden comb used to spread the warp across the loom (p. 30).

'Raddling': The process of separating and spreading the warp on the loom (p. 49).

Reed: A kind of steel comb used to control the spacing of the warp threads in the weave (p. 19).

Reed Hook: A tool used to draw the warp threads through the dents of the reed (p. 30).

'Reeding': The process of drawing the warp threads through the dents of the reed (p. 55).

Roller Cloth: A length of cloth fastened to the warp and cloth beams and to which the ends of the warp are attached.

'Rolling On': The mounting of the warp on to the warp roller (p. 50).

Rolling-on Sticks: Wooden laths used to separate the layers of warp on the warp roller so as to prevent them from cutting into each other (p. 30).

Röllakan: An interlock technique used to form geometrical designs on a tabby base (p. 74).

Rya: Scandinavian version of the tufted rug, generally having rather long tufts (p. 93).

Shafts: Wooden laths carrying the heddles (p. 23).

Shed: Separation of the warp threads so as to form an opening through which the weft can be passed (p. 16).

Shed Sticks: Two long wooden laths which are inserted at the crosses in the warp in order to maintain them during the threading-up process (p. 30).

Short Pile Method: A method of tufting rugs in which a continuous weft yarn is used instead of cut lengths (p. 91).

Shot: The passing of the shuttle through the shed.

Shuttles: Various shaped accessories used to carry the weft (p. 32).

Skein: A hank of wool yarn.

Snitch-Knot: An adjustable knot used by weavers (p. 56).

Slarvtjäll: The Scandinavian name for an inlay technique (p. 86).

Spool Holder or Rack: A rectangular frame for holding spools while warping (p. 29).

Tabby: Plain weave (p. 64).

Take-up: The shortening in length and width which occurs in the weave when the loom tension is taken off (p. 44).

Template or Stretcher: An accessory for keeping the weave width uniform (p. 34). Also a measure made of stiff paper or cardboard for accurate reproduction of pattern areas (p. 81).

Thread-up: The distribution of the warp threads between the shafts to produce, in combination with the pedal tie-up, a particular weave pattern (p. 60).

'Threading up': The process of passing each warp thread through the heddle eyes (p. 54).

Tie-up: The final stage in dressing of the loom, consisting of tying of the shafts and pedals (p. 55).

Tufted Rug: Rug with a raised pile surface (p. 87).

Turkish or Ghiordes Knot: A method of securing the tufts in a tufted rug (p. 88).

Underslung Loom: A type of loom on which the batten is pivoted from the base instead of being suspended from the upper frame (p. 20).

Upright Loom: A simple type of loom having only two shafts, sometimes provided with pedals and sometimes operated by hand (p. 21).

Warp: The threads running lengthways on the loom and into which the weft is woven (p. 15).

Warp Beam: Rear upper cross-piece of Horizontal Loom (p. 144).

Warping Board: A wooden board fitted with adjustable pegs and used to lay the warp (p. 30).

Warp Chain: Warp removed from warping board or mill and looped to prevent tangling (p. 48).

Warp Face Rug: A type of rug in which the pattern is formed by the warp (p. 75).

Warping Mill: A skeleton frame used for the same purpose as the warping board, but speedier in action and capable of taking larger warps (p. 29)

Weft: The threads or yarn crossing a weave from selvedge to selvedge (p. 15).

Index

The numerals in *italics* refer to the figure numbers of the line illustrations in the text; those in **heavy type** refer to the plate numbers of the halftone illustrations.

Accessories, 29
Additional cross, 46
Axminster carpet yarn, 38

Back roller stick, 50
Barbour's Champion Seaming Grey, 127
Basic weave, 63
Batten, 16, 19, 148
  beam, 49
  breast, 28, 53, 55
Beam, batten, 49
  breast, 28, 53, 55
  cloth, 55
Beaming on, 49
Beater, 16, 148
Beautlich, Tadek, 141
Board, warping, 45
Breast, batten, 28
  beam, 28, 53, 55
Broken heddle, 81

Calculation of quantities, 43
Camel hair yarn, 38
Carpet yarn, Axminster, 38
Castles, 32, 54, 56; *10*
Chain stitch, 91
  knot, 91
Chaining the warp, 48; **18**
Chequered rug in rosepath and tabby, 136
Cheviot wools, 35
Cloth beam, 55
  roller, 23, 58, 87
  stick, 49, 50

Colours in rag rugs, 82
  neutral, 102
Cops, 29, 45
Count of yarns, 43
Counts for wollen yarns, 44
Craftsman's Mark, Ltd., 37, 43, 108, 113,
      119, 127, 133, 135, 138, 141
Cross, additional, 46
Cross-bars, 46
Cross-pieces, 144
Cut length tufting, 88

Dacron, 40
Dentage, 28
Design, 101
Dollies, 32
Double warp, 47
  weave, 76; **46, 47**
  rug in, 135
Double woven rugs, 76
Dowel sticks, 58
Draft reading, 63
Drafts, 66
Dryad Handicrafts, Ltd., 38, 108, 111, 131
  warp string, 107

Experimental rug using twist method, 118

Fents, 40
Finishing off, 95
Fleece, 44
Floor loom, 19
Flossa, imitation, **42**
  rug, imitation, 93
  rugs, 93

Fringe, plain knotted, 95
Frühoff, Marlene, 109, 135
Furniture advert inspiration for design,
   30, 31

Gauge, tufting, 33, 34, 87, 88; *13*
Ghiordes knot, 88, 91
Goose-eye, 67; **61**
  sample weave in, 111
  weave, 111
Grierson, Ronald, 91, 127

Hair in rug weaving, 39
Heddle, 16, 24, 28, 54, 55; *5*; **4**
  broken, 81
  horses, 55, 56
  shafts, 23, 49, 55, 56; **4**
Heddleboard, 24; *5*
Heddles, threading the, 58
Hemp, plumbers, 37
Honeycomb weave, 69
  wool rug in, 114; **26-8**
Hook, reed, 30, 55; *9*
Horizontal overslung loom, 19, 22; **2**
  underslung loom, 19, 22; *3*
Horsehair, 39
Horses, heddle, 55, 56
Hutton, Helen, 107, 113, 119, 136, 138
  John, 138

Imitation *Flossa* rug, 93; **42**
Inlay, **34-6**
Interlock rug, 32; **31**

Jacobs, Young & Westbury, Ltd., 40, 110
Jaspe effect, 73

Kensington Weavers, Ltd., 131
"Key to Weaving", 63
Khelim interlock, **31**
  method, 119
  technique, 74
  pattern weaving, 21
  rug, 32, 119, 141
Kneebar, 55

Knight, Brian, 131
Knot, chain stitch, 91
  ghiordes, 88, 91
  reef, 55; *17a*
  Soumak stitch, 91
  Turkish, 88
Knotted fringe, plain, 95
Knotting in tufting weaving, 88

Lams, 24, 55, 56, 58, 64, 149; *6*
Laying the warp, 45
Leash, 21
Lewes, Klares, 108, 114, 121, 123, 133
Linen rug warp, 37, 38, 43
Linen Thread Co. Ltd., 38, 108, 110,
   111, 112, 117, 121, 123, 125, 131,
   136
Loom, home-made, 143
  horizontal, 19, 22; *3*
  floor, 19
  four-shaft, six-pedal, *6*
  overslung, 19; **2**
  preparing the, 45
  rug frame, 21, 22; *4*
  table, 19
  underslung, 19; *3*
  upright, 21; **3**

Mat, rush, 109
Meurling, Anne, 127, 137
Mill, Warping, 45
Moorhouse, Rodney, 107
Mullins, Barbara, 141
  Mrs. E. G., 138
Multicoloured warp, 47
Multiple Fabric Co. Ltd., 38, 39, 108,
   118

Natural green rush plait, 40
Navajo Indians, weaving by, 16
Neutral colours, 102
Norwegian weaves, 74, 75
Nylon, 40

Overslung loom, 19; **2**
Overshot pattern, 93

Part-tufted rug, 107
Parrey Cross, 46; **16**
Patten, Mary, 128
Pattern weaving, 63
Patterns in design, 103
Pavement inspiration for design, **48, 49**
Pedal tie-up, 28
Pedals, 55, 58, 64, 149; *6*
Pedalling, 94
Plain knotted fringe, 95
Plait, natural green rush, 40
Plaiting, three row, 97
Plumber's hemp, 37
Poor shed, 81
Porrey Cross, 46, 47, 49, 53
Portees, 50
Pulleys, 55, 56

Quantities, calculation of, 43

Raddle, 49, 54, 55
    top bar, 49, 50
Raddling, 49; **20**
Rag rugs, 40, 82, 86
    rug in tabby and rosepath, 121
        weave in twill, 110
        with inlay pattern, 123, 125
Reed, 16, 19, 23, 28, 49; **21**
    hook, 30, 55; *9*
Reeding, 55
Reef knot, 55; *17a*
Rib, weft, 75
Rollaken technique, 74, 75
Roller, 147
    cloth, 23, 58, 87; **6**
    stick, 23
        back, 50
Rolling-on, 50
    sticks, 30
Rosepath and tabby, **32**
    chequered rug in, 136; **48, 49**
    weave, 67, 86, 112
    wool rug in, 113; **29**
Rug frame, 93
    loom, 21, 22; *4*

imitation *flossa*, 93
in double weave, 135
interlock, 32
Khelim, 32, 119, 141
linen warp, 108
part-tufted, 107
tapestry, 137
    and tufted, 127
tufted hemp, 107
weaving, hair in, 39
wool, 108
Rugs, double-woven, 76
    Flossa, 93
    rag, 40, 82, 86
    Rya, 93
    tufted, 87
Rush mats, 39, 109
Rya rug, 93, 127, 131, 138; **39, 43**

Sample rag rug weave in twill, 110
    rug weave with spot pattern
        variant, 121
    wool rug weave, 108
    warp-faced weave, 107
    weave in goose-eye, 111
        imitation *Flossa*, 132
        rosepath and tabby, 112
Scandinavian peasant designs, 67
Section of shed, *2*
Selvedge, wavy, 80
Serge, 67
Shafts, 58, 149; *6, 24*; **4, 23**
    Heddle, 23, 49, 54, 55, 56; **4**
Shed, 34, 58; *2*
    poor, 81
    stick, 21, 30, 49, 50, 54, 58
Short pile method, 91
Shuttles, 32; *11*
Side frames, 143
Skein winder, 33; *7*
Skeins in cotton, 43
Slarvtjäll weave, 86
Snitch knots, 56, 58
Soumak stitch, 91
Southwick & Case, Ltd., 38, 40
Spool holder, 29, 45; *7, 29*; **8**
    winder, 32, 33; *12*

Spot pattern in a weave, 79; **25**
Stick, cloth, 49, 50
  roller, 23
Sticks, dowel, 58
  rolling-on, 30
Stitch, chain, 91
Stoddarts of Halifax, 38
Stone wall inspiration for design, **26–8**
Straub, Marianne, 128
Stuart, J. & W., Ltd., 38
Swedish slarvtjäll weave, 86
  weave, 74, 75

Tabby thread-up, 54
  weave, 16, 21, 23, 58, 60, 63, 64, 75,
    79, 85, 86, 112; *1*; **24, 32, 48, 49**
    alternative, 65
    wool rug in, 113; **29**
Table loom, 19
Take-up of warp, 44
Tapestry and tufted rug, 127
  rug, 137
Template, 34; *15*
Terylene, 40
Texture, 102
Threading the heddles, 58
Thread-up, 28, 54, 60, 67, 70
Threads crossed, 58
Three row plaiting, 98
Throwing, uneven, 50
Tie-up, 55, 64, 70, 79, 94
Tone, 101
Top-bar, raddle, 49, 50
Tufted hemp rug, 107; **11**
  rugs, 87, 128, 133; **37, 38, 40, 41, 44,
    45**
Tufting, cut length, 88
  gauge, 33, 34, 87, 88; *13*
Turkish knot, 88
Twill, 66
  weave, 67, 86; **22**
Twist method, experimental rug using,
  118

Underslung loom, 19; *3*

Uneven throwing, 80
  warp tension, 80
Upright loom, 21; **3**

Volcanic pools inspiration for design, **44,
  45**

Waisted weave, 34; *14*
Wall inspiration for design, **26–8**
Warp, 15, 28, 37, 58
  and weft rug, 'Black and White'. 141
  chaining the, 48; **18**
  double, 47
  faced rug, 37, 75
  face technique, 54
  faced weave, 10
  laying the, 45
  linen rug, 37, 38, 43
  multi-coloured, 47
  rug linen, 108
  string, 45
  take-up of, 44
  tension, uneven, 80
  thread, broken, 81
  threads, 55
  wastage of, 100
Warping board, 29, 45; *8a, 8b*
  mill, 29, 45; **9**
Wavy selvedge, 80
Weave, basic, 63
  double, 76; **47**
  honeycomb, 69; **28**
  Norwegian, 74, 75
  pattern, 60
    varieties, 63
  rosepath, 67, 86
  sample wool rug, 108
  structure, 70
  Swedish slarvtjäll, 86
  tabby, 21, 23, 70, 75, 85, 86
  twill, 86
  warp-faced, 107; **10**
Weaver's Shop Ltd., 38
Weaving, basic principles, 60
  pattern, 63
  short pile, 91

Weft, 15
  calculation, 44
  materials, 38
  rib, 75
Welsh wools, 38
Wilton Royal Carpet Factory, 38
Winder, spool, 32, 33; *12*
Wool gauge, 88
  rug, 108
    in honeycomb weave, 114
    rosepath and tabby, 113

Wollen warp, 1
  yarns, counts for, 44
Wools, Cheviot, 35
World Fair, 40
Woven rug, 37, **38**
'Woven Rugs', 91

Yarn, Axminster carpet, 38
  camel hair, 38
Yarns, count of, 43

Zigzag design, **33**